What's Your Anger Type? Revised Edition

with

Technological Rage: Millennial Anger

Peter Andrew Sacco PH.D.

Copyright © 2016 Peter Sacco

PAPERBACK ISBN: 978-1-63491-161-0

All rights reserved. No part of this publication may be reproduced, stored in a retrieval system, or transmitted, in any form or by any means, electronic, mechanical, photocopying, recording or otherwise, without the prior permission of the publishers.

Published by BookLocker.com, Inc., Bradenton, Florida, U.S.A.

Printed on acid-free paper.

BookLocker.com, Inc.
2016

First Edition

Edited by Thomas L. Law III & Wanda Tyler

Peter Sacco asserts the moral right to be identified as the author of this work

Disclaimer

This book details the author's personal experiences with and opinions about anger management. The author is not a licensed psychologist.

The author and publisher are providing this book and its contents on an "as is" basis and make no representations or warranties of any kind with respect to this book or its contents. The author and publisher disclaim all such representations and warranties, including for example warranties of merchantability and psychological advice for a particular purpose. In addition, the author and publisher do not represent or warrant that the information accessible via this book is accurate, complete or current.

The statements made about products and services have not been evaluated by the U.S. government. Please consult with your own legal or accounting professional regarding the suggestions and recommendations made in this book.

Except as specifically stated in this book, neither the author or publisher, nor any authors, contributors, or other representatives will be liable for damages arising out of or in connection with the use of this book. This is a comprehensive limitation of liability that applies to all damages of any kind, including (without limitation) compensatory; direct, indirect or consequential damages; loss of data, income or profit; loss of or damage to property and claims of third parties.

You understand that this book is not intended as a substitute for consultation with a licensed medical, legal or accounting professional. Before you begin any change your lifestyle in any way, you will consult a licensed professional to ensure that you are doing what's best for your situation.

This book provides content related to anger management topics. As such, use of this book implies your acceptance of this disclaimer.

About the Author

Dr. Peter Sacco has been working with individuals in private practice and support groups for over a decade. He specializes in anger-management classes, workshops/seminars, individual coaching and counseling.

As a professor, he teaches at universities and colleges in the United States and Canada. He teaches courses in addiction studies, police studies, criminal psychology, and education.

Peter also produces television shows and hosts Canada's most popular radio show on mental health *MATTERS OF THE MIND*. He is an award-winning executive producer.

To learn more about Peter and his work, or to book him for a speaking engagement, please visit his website:

www.petersacco.com

Other Titles by Peter Sacco

Fast Food Dating Your 2 Cents
Why Women Want What They Can't Have
Penis Envy
Breast Envy
The Internet Apocalypse

Acknowledgements

Thank you to all of the individuals who I have spoken with over the 'decades' who have shared their insights and ideas about anger. Thank you to the news talk radio and television shows who have entrusted me to come on their shows and share my knowledge and wisdom over the last 20 years!

Contents

FORWARD .... **xiii**

PRAISE FROM SOMEONE IN RECOVERY .... **xvii**

SECTION 1- WHAT'S YOUR ANGER TYPE? REVISED

1 - An Informal Introduction to Your Anger 1
2 - And Your Anger Type is? 9
3 - Resistant and Passive Anger 21
4 - Internet and Computer Rage 31
5 - Addictive Anger 37
6 - Petrified Anger 45
7 - Compressive Anger 55
8 - Jealousy 63
9 - Road Rage 71
10 - Conflictual Anger 81
11 - Habitual Anger 89
12 - Passive-Aggression 97
13 - Moralistic Anger 105
14 - Manipulative Anger 115
15 - What Motivates Your Anger? 125
16 - Angry Personalities 135
17 - How To Manage Your Anger 159

18 - Children and Anger 187
19 - Tired of Fighting? 195

SECTION 2- TECHNOLOGICAL RAGE: MILENNIAL ANGER

TEXTING TORMENT 215
ONLINE SOCIAL NETWORKING 229
CYBERDATING 245

References 259
Recommended Readings 263
Other books by Peter Sacco 265

FORWARD

I believe the time was right to re-release this book, adding a whole new section on "technological rage". Since writing this book over a decade ago, it seems that destructive anger has not only grown worse, but it has evolved with technology. In the last five years, I have been contacted by many radio and television networks to appear on their shows as an expert to discuss anger, what causes it, why it escalates into rage, and what can be done to help those with severe anger management problems.

Each time you turn on the television, or see what is trending on Facebook, your stomach turns as you read about another school shooting, an act of domestic terrorism in some workplaces, or a violent act of terrorism perpetrated by an international terrorist organization. Are people really becoming that much angrier that they believe that they need to engage in acts of evil and murder? It really does make you shake your head and wonder! I have been asked on many occasions, "Can anger be addictive?" After working with individuals one on one in counseling and in groups for many years, I would definitely have to say "yes"!

There are people who get totally aroused, empowered and motivated by their anger. According to Hans Seyle, the creator of the "Fight or Flight" response phenomenon, people respond to adversity and emotions in one of two ways. They either run from it, or they stand up to it. If you keep standing up to conflict or seek it, you get aroused and release adrenaline. This hormone provides a rush almost like a stimulant or "upper". After a while, some people get aroused by this feeling so much, they need it. You see it in sports where aggression is a requirement or by-product for success (i.e., football, boxing, UFC, hockey). They use their anger which moves them toward action.

I have found in clients I have worked with who possess this type of anger when they are not engaging in conflict or getting angry, they get bored and/or sometimes even depressed. I have had some clients with alcohol addictions tell me they go to bars on weekends hoping to get into fights. This provides them with both a sense of excitement and power. Just as drugs provide someone with excitement and power, anger can become the same kind of stimulant.

There are so many different types of anger and many reasons why people develop them. There are also many different types of addictions and many reasons why people become addicted to substances. There is, however, an underlying basic root or component which manifests something as addictive and why the addiction is maintained. That root is low self-esteem. To some degree, we all go through bouts of doubt in ourselves which can trigger feelings of low self-esteem. Most of us find ways to adapt and modify our self-concept so we can feel good again.

There are some people whose self-concept is so low they become depressed and stay in that mood/mindset. Some experts would assert that depression is actually anger turned inward. I would agree with this when an individual demonstrates masochistic traits and self-destructive tendencies. Those who display their depression outward and become aggressive may actually be masking their depression with anger. Anger becomes a coping mechanism. Just as some people use drugs and alcohol to cope, some people use anger the same way. This becomes their vice!

I could spend hours discussing the intricacies of anger, but here is what I think the two most important attributes of anger are to keep in mind: (1) Everyone gets angry as it is a normal and healthy emotion, and (2) You are not nuts or insane when you get angry.

It is how you deal with your anger which is the most important factor going forward. Your response can be one that is controlled or one that is out of control and very destructive!

What can you do to change yourself? Practicing patience, seeking guidance/help and renewing the spirit of your mind is a great start! You also have to recondition your thinking and reacting. When we become conditioned to respond angrily, we develop a tendency to respond to most, if not all, similar situations the same way. In essence, you shortcut your thought processes and put your minds on automatic pilot. Rather than rationalize the experience before responding, you react in a conditioned manner. You have to become more introspective of your emotions and learn what sets you off. What are your triggers?

You have to assume responsibility for your actions and reactions. Identify those certain people or situations that set you off and prepare to deal with them differently. There are excellent anger management tools to help you identify your triggers and how to respond differently. The key to change starts with your willingness to accept that you have an anger management problem.

The book *What's Your Anger Type?* has been published on four continents, used in colleges and universities as a text book, used in support groups, and has been read by thousands of people worldwide. Many people who have read this book and used the anger management tools in it, claim it has not only changed their lives, but has also saved them from embarrassment, legal problems, from getting fired at work, and even prevented their marriages/families from falling apart!

The purpose of this book is not to chastise you, or tell you what you are doing wrong. Instead, it is about how to make things right in your life when it comes to dealing with emotions that seem to be getting the better of you. My goal is to help teach you how to live a happier and more productive life.

May you move forward letting cooler heads prevail!

Blessings,

Peter Andrew Sacco Ph.D.

PRAISE FROM SOMEONE IN RECOVERY

What's Your Anger Type? is a very informative, enlightening, educational, and entertaining book that sheds tremendous light on the whole emotion of anger. I strongly recommend this book for anyone dealing with their own personal anger-management issues, or living with those possessing anger-management problems.

I am an individual who has dealt with her own fair share of anger issues, which were a bi-product of my addiction/use and recovery. The concepts and strategies in this book helped me not only with my anger-management and aggression issues, but also with my recovery for substance abuse. It helped me understand why I was angry, why I carried a chip on both shoulders and then to come up with ways for creating positive change in my life.

Whether you are young or old, male or female, Western or Eastern culture, this book will definitely help you if you apply the principles that Peter teaches. If you are a parent or a teacher, I would highly recommend this book if you have a short fuse around children. I know my anger types, now I hope you find yours and achieve something positive.

Good luck!

Andrea P.
Toronto, Canada

1

An Informal Introduction to Your Anger

In the beginning the universe was created.
This has made a lot of people angry and been
widely regarded as a bad move.

Douglas Adams

Do you have an anger-management problem? Is there something or someone around you, or in your life who is always getting under your skin? Do you just want to explode? Do you feel like you are at the end of your "anger control leash"?

If you answered yes to any of these questions, then this book can definitely help. It might even save you from detrimental situations!

Let's face it, everyone gets angry. Anger is a normal and acceptable human emotion just as happiness, joy, surprise, sadness, and angst. Unfortunately, most of the time anger is expressed in non-productive and unacceptable ways.

No one really complains about individuals who are happy all the time. Similarly, most wouldn't be insensitive to individuals who are experiencing bouts of sadness. Why then is anger looked at in a less productive light?

Perhaps it is due to the few isolated incidents that make the news and media because someone has behaved so badly when they were enraged. Maybe it could be due to the urban legends/myths of people becoming "superhuman" monsters during fits of rage!

Could it be how movies and television portray anger and vengeance for wrongdoings? How far will people go when they are angry? Could they really lose it mentally, psychology and emotionally when they become enraged? Have you ever experienced meltdown?

Interestingly, everyone has the ability to control all facets of how they act, including their anger, because we can all control the seeds that start the process – our *thoughts*!

Below is the flowchart I use with clients to explain how and why they become angry. I will explain it in greater detail later in the book. For now, just examine briefly the process of how our anger begins, flourishes and ends.

Think angry --- Feel angry --- Act angry --- Become angry

In short, thoughts determine your emotions, even anger.

☼

Throughout this book I will present 10 key points that I hope will assist you in your anger-management:

1. If we think it, we'll feel it, we'll act that way, and over a long period of time we may even take on that behavior and become it – an angry person.
2. Anger is a normal and healthy emotion. All people emote and are capable of becoming angry at any point in their lives.
3. Since we are all able to exert control over our emotions, we can determine how we choose to express our anger.
4. Anger is a secondary emotion. Some other emotion or thought process always comes *before* anger.
5. There are 12 types of anger and most of us possess some, even many, in different situations and periods in our lives.
6. Everyone possesses a distinct behavioral style for dealing with the world and people around us.
7. There are ways of managing and controlling your anger in more effective and productive ways if you are willing to work at it.
8. It's never too late to modify negative, destructive expressions of anger and replace them with optimal, acceptable alternatives.
9. The same rules for managing anger apply to everyone, even children.
10. It's okay to laugh at yourself sometimes.

In a Sentence or Two, What bothers you Most?

Before delving any further into this book, I'd like you to spend a few minutes, or longer if required, to make a casual self-inventory of your anger.

Pay close attention to all the specific people, places, situations, and things that contribute to your anger. List anything and everything you can think of, no matter how foolish or absurd it may appear.

Things that anger me most are...

1.

2.

3.

4.

5.

6.

7.

8.

9.

10.

Now that you have listed your top 10 anger precipitators, compare them with the most common irritants that people report. As you look through the list, see if you can pick out a common theme.

Common Anger Triggers:

1. Spouse
2. Children
3. Co-workers
4. Boss
5. Traffic
6. Rude people
7. Dogs pooping on your lawn
8. Bad weather (too much rain/snow)
9. Governments and politicians
10. Taxes
11. Long line-ups
12. Bad drivers
13. Inflation
14. Drunk people
15. Gossipers
16. Slow restaurant service
17. Congested parking lots
18. Messy kids/spouses
19. People who cheat
20. Sports teams you root for that always lose
21. Bad parents
22. Rules that make no sense
23. Racism/discrimination
24. TV/cable problems
25. Bad Internet service
26. People talking during movies
27. Obnoxious sports fans
28. People who let you down
29. Plans that fall through/disappointment
30. People abusing the social assistance/support system
31. Tardiness in others
32. Self
33. When life treats you unfairly

34. Stupidity
35. Barking dogs
36. Babies crying uncontrollably
37. Hard to follow directions/instructions
38. People smoking in your space
39. Ban on smoking (for smokers)
40. People who stand/sit too close, invading your personal space
41. When someone wakes you up
42. Telemarketers
43. Door-to-door solicitors
44. When someone doesn't listen to you or understand you
45. Litter bugs
46. People who don't flush toilets/urinals
47. Road construction
48. Trains holding up traffic
49. Plane delays
50. Things/cars breaking down

How many "irritants" on the list were you able to relate too as "triggers" for your own anger?

Throughout this book I will use these two terms "irritants" and "triggers" to refer to those people, events or things you attribute to causing you to experience anger. Also, I will show you how nothing can make you angry unless you allow it that power. Even though something from the above list can attribute to your anger, it can't make you angry!

Nothing can make you angry on its own unless you let it!

When you look at the title of this book *What's Your Anger Type?* you're probably asking yourself is there more than one type of anger, and if so what type(s) of anger do I have?

Identifying what type of anger you possess is probably the best place to start. Once you identify your anger type, then you can identify your triggers/irritants and modify behaviors, situations and perceptions to create new ways of feeling.

2

And Your Anger Type is?

The biggest misconception about me is that I'm angry and violent. But I'm a real sweetie.

Jack Nicholson

Want to Know What Your Anger Type Is?

If you want to know more about what type of anger you possess, it would be a good idea to complete the modified questionnaire below. It has been developed from hundreds of sample questions given to clients, patients, students, employee program participants, and general interest groups.

The outcome of the questionnaire will show you what types of anger exist and which one(s) you possess. In subsequent chapters I will provide explanations and descriptions of each anger type.

I have selected the best 36 questions that illuminate specific anger types. You will need a pen or pencil. On a separate sheet of paper, make a list from 1 to 36. For each question, write down the corresponding score that best represents how you are feeling, thinking or behaving in that particular situation.

0 - Does Not Pertain To Me
1 - Sometimes True For Me

3 - Often The Case For Me
5 - Always The Case For Me

When completing this quiz, it is very important to think about your answers in the present moment. Do not answer questions based on how you once behaved or how you wish you behaved.

The best way to determine your particular anger type(s) is to be as honest as possible and give yourself the rating that first comes to mind. Do not rationalize or think too much about each question.

Also, do not get worried if you feel you are answering too many questions as "most of the time". The purpose of this quiz is not to diagnose but to identify anger patterns and types in order to make appropriate thought, feeling and behavior modifications.

What's Your Anger Type? Quiz

Q1. No matter what the situation is, I try to never get mad. To get mad would not be good.

      0   1   3   5

Q2. Whenever my computer screen freezes up I pound on the mouse. I don't have time for this!

      0   1   3   5

Q3. I like getting angry because it really pumps me up. I feel like I can do anything when I am angry.

      0   1   3   5

Q4. When I get angry I stay angry for a long time. It's just so hard to let it go.

      0   1   3   5

Q5. I tend to really lose emotional control when I get mad. I just can't think rationally.

      0   1   3   5

Q6. In my relationships I tend to get jealous quite easily.

      0   1   3   5

Q7. I tend to get really annoyed whenever I get stuck in traffic jams. I have no patience.

      0   1   3   5

Q8. I find myself easily getting into arguments and debates with others over trivial things.

      0   1   3   5

Q9. There is rarely a day that goes by in which I don't get mad.

      0   1   3   5

Q10. When I am angry I usually like to hide my feelings and pretend I am not angry.

      0   1   3   5

Q11. I really get upset whenever someone puts me down or insults me.

      0   1   3   5

Q12. I am most motivated whenever I am angry. My anger moves me toward action.

      0   1   3   5

Q13. I feel very uncomfortable whenever I am faced with confrontations or conflicts. I try to avoid them.

0   1   3   5

Q14. I get so angry when I get pop ups on my Internet. I curse and swear. Damn advertisements!

0   1   3   5

Q15. Watching fights in sports, on television or in real life excites me. I actually get pumped up!

0   1   3   5

Q16. Forgiving others who have wronged me is very difficult. I just can't seem to forgive and forget.

0   1   3   5

Q17. The best way to describe me when I am mad is a time bomb. I get so angry I explode!

0   1   3   5

Q18. I tend to have a habit of putting people down behind their backs.

0   1   3   5

Q19. Whenever someone cuts me off when I am driving, I curse them with fingers or fist gestures and yell at them.

0   1   3   5

Q20. I like to prepare for an argument with someone even

though they have no idea it is coming. I argue to win!

    0   1   3   5

Q21. I am angry most of the time throughout the course of a day. This seems to be a common feeling I experience

    0   1   3   5

Q22. I don't get mad... I prefer to get even!

    0   1   3   5

Q23. Whenever I discuss my personal beliefs or ideals, I find myself defending them aggressively. If people don't like what I think or believe, then to heck with them!

    0   1   3   5

Q24. I find when I am angry I can get what I want much easier. My anger gets me what I want!

    0   1   3   5

Q25. I have always been taught anger is bad and I should never show it.

    0   1   3   5

Q26. Nothing annoys me more than telemarketers. What gives them the right to call my house?

    0   1   3   5

Q27. Whenever I or someone around me gets angry, I get

really excited. My heart races and I feel things getting out of control.

      0   1   3   5

Q28. I tend to relive the wrongs people have done to me over and over in my head. I just can't shake these thoughts!

      0   1   3   5

Q29. When I get angry I punch, throw or break things.

      0   1   3   5

Q30. I dislike people who get everything they want in life. Why does everyone else get the breaks?

      0   1   3   5

Q31. When people in front of me drive too slow, I get angry. They shouldn't be driving if they don't drive the speed limit!

      0   1   3   5

Q32. I tend to find fault with people and things in life. I just wish things would be more the way I would like them to be.

      0   1   3   5

Q33. I have dreams in which I get into fights and come out the winner. I like these kinds of dreams because they make me feel good even though they are not real.

      0   1   3   5

Q34. If someone has hurt me or wronged me, I will see to it they experience the same kind of hurt as well.

      0   1   3   5

Q35. I can't talk about politics, religion or personal subjects without feeling myself getting upset or even angry. These types of topics should not be discussed as they only lead to disagreements.

      0   1   3   5

Q36. I tend to work best under stress and pressure. I prefer deadlines because I seem to always get things done at the last minute.

      0   1   3   5

END OF QUIZ

Please tally your score (the numbers you circled). Once you have a total, compare it with the following measures:

150 - 180 points	Severe Anger Management Problems
120 - 149 points	Moderate Anger Management Problems
80 - 119 points	Mild Anger Management Problems
30 - 79 points	Stressed/Frustrated Easily
0 - 29 points	Cool As A Cucumber

☼

If you had a score that was extremely high (the severe anger-management domain), don't fret. I will provide you with the necessary tools for dealing with your anger later in the book.

For now though, it's not your total score you'll focus on, rather the subset scores that match up to each specific category of anger.

There are 12 types of anger you were tested for. Your anger usually falls within one of these 12 types. In order to better understand which specific type of anger you possess, please re-tally your scores using the following method.

Add your scores combining the questions in the following groups:

Subgroups

1	Questions: 1, 13, 25
2	Questions: 2, 14, 26
3	Questions: 3, 15, 27
4	Questions: 4, 16, 28
5	Questions: 5, 17, 29
6	Questions: 6, 18, 30
7	Questions: 7, 19, 31
8	Questions: 8, 20, 32
9	Questions: 9, 21, 33
10	Questions: 10, 22, 34
11	Questions: 11, 23, 35
12	Questions: 12, 24, 36

For each subgroup, you will have a different score. Each score will represent a specific type of anger.

Once you have a score for each subgroup, please compare the score with the matching measures:

Measures
12 - 15	Very High
9 - 11	High
5 - 8	Moderate
1 - 4	Low

If your score for the 3 questions in each subgroup tallies "Very High" or "High", then you possess the characteristics for that specific type of anger. Generally, most people score highly in more than just one category.

The following subgroups of questions reflect a particular anger type:

Subgroup Anger Type
1	Resistant/Passive
2	Internet/Computer Rage
3	Addictive Anger
4	Petrified Anger
5	Compressive Anger
6	Jealousy
7	Road Rage
8	Conflictual Anger
9	Habituated Anger
10	Passive-Aggression
11	Moralistic Anger
12	Manipulative Anger

Each of the subtypes of anger possesses an "anger component" at the core of the domain. However, there are different reasons for how the anger evolved and why it continues.

In the subsequent chapters, I will provide a working definition of each type of anger focusing on its beginnings, it's M.O. (method of operation) and its typical outcome.

Keep in mind, the type of anger you possess may change or shift depending on the events taking place in your life. Also, since most of us experience stress and frustration as a by-product of the busy lives we lead, it would be expected that we would experience some type of anger some of the time.

Let's now discuss each anger type in turn.

3

Resistant and Passive Anger

If you kick a stone in anger, you'll hurt your own foot.

Korean Proverb

When you were a child, did your parents ever tell you anger is "bad" and you should never show it? Were you ever punished for getting upset and then banished to your bedroom, or if in school, to the corner? Perhaps your parents were of the mindset "children should be seen and not heard"?

If you scored "High" or "Very High" for the questions pertaining to resistant/passive anger, then you may have issues with anger as an emotion!

Resistant/passive anger is the type of anger learned from parents, role models and teachers who lack emotional expression or dismiss anger as a healthy emotion.

In fact, this type of anger is passed on from generation to generation by those who are averse to expressing emotions they view as negative. They also try to avoid all forms of conflict in their lives. They endorse an affirmation that "anger is bad" and should be avoided at all times.

Some families and cultures view the expression of anger as a weakness! They believe when one expresses emotions such as anger and sadness, they are revealing their psychological weaknesses.

Moreover, media (TV shows and movies) usually portray angry people as explosive and out of control. Some movies have gone so far as to depict anger as a mental health illness requiring committal to a psychiatric ward or serious on-going counseling. Is it any wonder some people avoid the issue of anger all together?

A major reason resistant/passive anger manifests in people is because they've been raised in dysfunctional families where fighting was a normal event. When you were a child growing up, did your parents and family members argue and fight all the time? Did the constant fighting give you butterflies and make your stomach upset? Did you worry someone was going to get hurt? Perhaps you? Did family members go to bed with anger weighing heavy in their hearts?

You might have felt so sad and helpless from the bickering and fighting that you just withdrew. You may have felt totally helpless and made a conscious promise to yourself never to get angry or disagree with anyone because it might lead to fighting.

The groundwork was laid and you trained your mind to avoid anger at all costs by keeping everything inside. This is not healthy! Did you know that anger turned inward and never expressed has the ability to take on a detrimental emotion called depression?

If you keep everything inside yourself and never vent your frustrations, these feelings are going to fester inside of you like some old cheese left in the back of the refrigerator.

In the beginning you know what anger is. The more you keep suppressing it, however, you lose track of what it becomes. It develops into a kind of disfigured entity like moldy cheese, which becomes discolored and hard to discern anymore. The longer it stays in the tray and cultures the more difficult it is to clean.

Oftentimes people suffering from depression will describe their moods as gray or black. That is what depression feels like for many, a dark pit! They feel helpless, hopeless and hapless. They feel they have little or no control over their lives. They feel ignored and no one cares.

Why is that? Because they don't dare speak up for fear they might offend, challenge or make someone angry! According to this type of anger, you must avoid anger at all costs, even if that means making yourself feel ill.

Here are some examples where resistant anger is at its worst.

☼

Scenario #1

Sandra is fed up with people using her. She feels like she is always giving to people but never getting anything in return.

One of her closest friends Amanda is the prime culprit. She feels Amanda takes advantage of her and uses her. She has a hard time saying "no" to Amanda's requests. She worries however, that if she refuses her Amanda might like her less or not want to be her friend at all.

This really bothers Sandra, yet she has made a conscious decision to be strong and say "no" next time Amanda asks her to babysit her kids.

A friend from Sandra's past calls and invites her to go to a concert this coming Friday night. Sandra is ecstatic and can't wait to go.

The next day Amanda calls and asks her to babysit the same night as the concert. Amanda tells her it is very important; she has the "dream date" of her life.

Sandra can hear the loud "no's" screaming in her head. Before she even knows what has happened, though, she has agreed to babysit Amanda's kids, thus forfeiting the Friday concert. She is so upset with Amanda. She hates Amanda! She hates herself for agreeing!

What is the cause of Sandra's anger? The inability to say no due to fear of rejection.

What are the precipitating factors? Others know they can take advantage of Sandra. They know exactly how much they can get away with. Sandra is a pleaser. Due to her low self-esteem, she worries that others will stop liking her.

Do these friends actually like and respect her?

Scenario #2

Ivan asks Nick if he wants to see a movie Saturday night. Nick's response is, "Yeah, if you want too."

Ivan asks Nick which movie he would like to see. "I don't know, whatever you want," replies Nick.

"Do you want me to pick you up or do you want to get me?" Ivan asks Nick. Nick shrugs his shoulders. "Doesn't matter to me."

Ivan asks Nick if he prefers to see the early show or the late show. "Either one is okay with me," replies Nick.

Ivan starts to feel very frustrated with Nick's indecisiveness. Nick on the other hand, feels pressured by Ivan. Ivan wishes he had never asked Nick to hang out with him in the first place.

What is the cause of Nick's resistant anger? He doesn't know how to make decisions for himself. He tends to go with the flow, never being the initiator.

What are the precipitating factors? Nick has probably had others make plans and decisions for him in the past. It is a good bet Nick has never been taught how to be assertive. In fact, his parents were probably over-protective.

Ivan on the other hand becomes frustrated and annoyed over Nick's indecisiveness. Nick perceives Ivan's invite as a burden, forcing him to make a decision.

Scenario #3

Kelly was taught by her parents at an early age little girls should be seen and not heard. As a 25-year old lady, she now works for a firm as a secretarial assistant. She feels her boss and other co-workers place unrealistic workloads on her desk, demands she is unable to meet.

Her boss has asked her on occasion if she would like an assistant to help her. She has blatantly refused to have an assistant, stating, "Everything is under control."

The stress from work is really getting to her. She rarely sleeps, eats and is miserable most of the time. She has grown to hate going to work. She resents her boss more each day.

Noticing her recent discomfort and unhappiness, her boss requests a meeting to discuss her mood swings. She assures her boss everything is fine and that it's a woman thing, not to worry.

He suggests bringing in an assistant and she argues she doesn't need one. In fact, she requests more work to take home for the weekend as she claims this is her passion. Her boss gives in to her requests.

Weeks later, while leaving work late one afternoon, she notices she has left her keys inside the car and the doors are locked. Kelly picks up a large brick and starts bashing in the driver's window before smashing all the windows. She cowers to the ground and begins to break down.

What is the cause of Kelly's anger? Being stressed and over-worked.

What are the precipitating factors? Kelly's main problem is that she doesn't know how to do things in moderation. She doesn't seek help when she needs it and refuses it when offered. She has learned to keep everything inside and not burden others.

Most importantly, Kelly does not have an outlet for her stress, thus leading to her emotional breakdown. She needs to learn to release the emotional garbage before it festers inside of her.

☼

Have you ever heard the term "nervous breakdown"?

Clinically speaking, there is no such thing. Perhaps the best way to refer to this loosely slung, slang term is to view it as mental burnout. The precipitating cause is persistent or escalating stress in one's life, which leads to unceasing frustration. Eventually, you get to the point where you can't take it anymore and reach meltdown.

Here are some of the signs and symptoms to look for with this type of anger:

- Chronic fatigue
- Nausea/vomiting
- Constant colds
- Small aches/pains
- Feeling tired and run down
- Loss of appetite

- Sleep disturbances/insomnia
- Mental flashbacks
- Frequent crying spells
- Suicidal thoughts
- Social isolation/withdrawing
- Drinking/drug use
- Pessimism
- Irrational fears
- Depression

Interestingly, depression seems to be the most common by-product of resistant anger. The individual is so pre-occupied with not being angry that they become highly focused on the emotion unconsciously.

Consequently, the anger is turned inward and manifests itself in the form of depression. Rather than expel the negative feelings that are building inside, you hold onto them and try to extinguish them inside. Sure the anger gets watered down; however, it becomes diluted into a more "acceptable" emotion – depression.

Think about it for a moment. What emotion is more likely to receive greater empathy and sympathy? Anger or depression?

If you're angry, people avoid you because they perceive you as dangerous. On the other hand, if you are depressed, you are perceived to be less of a threat. In fact, people will start to feel sorry for you and actually enable your depression. So you in fact become more readily "accepted" for being depressed.

Have you ever been around someone or know someone who constantly complains all the time? Are they always complaining about some ache or pain? Does it feel like pulling teeth whenever you ask them to make a decision or commit to something?

This resistant type of anger allows a person to engage in a passive, helpless mindset where they rely on others to make their decisions for them.

Some individuals with resistant anger could be classified as possessing a "sadomasochistic" personality. In fact, the only time they feel alive is when they are "in pain" or complaining about something.

From my work with clients, these are some of the behavioral attributes individuals with this anger type display:

- Allowing others to make decisions for them
- Feeling used and unappreciated
- Frustrating others by showing no initiative or assertion
- Saying yes when they want to say no
- Being in situations they don't want to be in
- Blaming others for their unhappiness
- Constantly seeking other's approval
- Feeling like every situation is the same

The bottom line with this anger type is they *never feel good about themselves*. The world is always unfair to them. They were dealt a bad hand of cards. There is a conspiracy going on and everyone is against them. They just don't understand why things are the way they are.

These people have developed a method of self-defeating thinking and have trapped themselves in a lazy, irrational, stereotypical way of perceiving the world.

I once spoke with Dr. Robert Schuller. He taught "possibility thinking" through his books and television show, *The Hour of Power*. I asked him what he thought were the most important needs a human possessed.

He told me: self-esteem.

Bottom line: People with resistant anger require assertiveness training and self-esteem growth.

4

Internet and Computer Rage

No man can think clearly when his fists are clenched.

George Jean Nathan

I am sure everyone reading this book uses a computer or has had at least one experience using a computer. Moreover, I am sure the majority of readers are connected to the Internet and surf the Web on a regular basis.

If you've just bought a computer, did you know it will become obsolete within a year? Just knowing that annoys the heck out of me!

The reason why computers become obsolete is because technology is changing so fast and the industry is trying to keep up with the relentless rat race. Guess who are the rats chasing the technological cheese?

That would be you and me! We have become part of the process, constantly trying to keep up and stay in sync with change.

Computer technology is very much like the fast food industry – I want it right here, right now! Most of us do not practice patience. The irony is that most industries and homes use computers to do tasks faster and more efficiently. The operative word is "faster". However, the problem now becomes: How fast is fast enough?

When I switched over from dial-up Internet to high-speed Internet. I was one of those archaic dial-up users who was too lazy to make the switch to high-speed. Colleagues and friends kept telling me "you're going to be amazed at the difference between dial-up and high-speed."

In fact, I was told: "You're going to tell yourself you should have switched much sooner once you see the difference!"

Guess what? I made the switch and they were right! The speed was incredible! However, there was one thing I was left to ponder. Several high-speed users were still complaining that things weren't fast enough.

Wow! For me, it was like comparing a ten-speed bicycle to a motorcycle. The differences in speed were obvious, yet they had now become desensitized to it and needed an even quicker Internet fix!

Internet speed freaks are one thing, but the Internet "ragers" are something else. They displace their dissatisfaction with the speed through forms of aggression and even violence.

Here are some of the most common symptoms of Internet rage I heard while researching this type of anger:

- You're waiting for the URL site to change and you're growing impatient

- Your screen freezes and you start pounding the mouse or keys
- Pop ups keep appearing on your screen and you start swearing
- Your e-mail is overloaded with junk mail and you start cursing
- Blind ads are sent to you and you actually reply with nasty e-mails
- You participate in Internet chat to precipitate arguments
- You constantly surf the Web to get your fix otherwise you get very irritable
- You start stalking others in chat rooms or through their e-mail
- You've actually punched your monitor when things were moving too slow or have frozen
- You've actually picked up the monitor and thrown it at the wall or out the window

☼

I recall one individual in anger-management counseling who was so irate when their screen froze that they picked up their monitor and threw it out a window of an office building. They forgot they were on one of the higher floors and nearly hit a pedestrian below!

Lack of Internet speed and slow computer function are the two most common complaints I hear in regard to computer anger. In fact, those who become aggressive over lack of computer speed only make matters worse when they pound the mouse or the keyboard. It just confuses the computer further and freezes it for longer, making them even angrier.

Some actually punch the older-style monitors, breaking fingernails and fingers!

A university professor colleague of mine teaching computer technology actually teaches her classes a "Must Hands Off" skill in the first lecture. She instructs students to guard against Internet rage by having them sit on their hands after clicking the mouse twice.

Anymore than twice, she asserts, is only risking a computer freeze and causing further frustration. "Hands under your glutes," is her favorite line!

It might be one of the harder things to do, resist the urge to click the heck out of the mouse. The constant clicking however becomes a precursor to your frustration and anger.

☼

Telemarketers

A similar frustrating technological irritant for many people is telemarketers, those who phone you at home and try to sell you something. What is it about telemarketers that upsets you?

Most agree they are just a nuisance. They hate being called at home and disturbed. I can buy that. If you are like me, your home is your private domain. I operate under the premise that if I want to purchase something I look it up in the yellow pages or on the Internet.

For some reason it seems telemarketer calls are on the rise, and I have even noticed an increasing number of calls to my house. This occurrence is something I don't get angry about or lose sleep over, as that would be foolish.

I believe if the callers are a major concern and you want to preserve whatever sanity you have left, then I suggest the following options I have learned from interviewing people and speaking to law enforcement officials:

- Change your phone number to an unlisted number
- Put a block on your phone for all unknown numbers
- Call the companies or clearing houses directly and ask that your number be taken off their lists
- Screen all your calls through call answer
- Screen all your calls through call display
- Politely tell marketers you are not interested
- If they are persistent and keep calling you back, speak another language if you can (cheeky, but I know someone who tried it and it worked!)

Getting flustered and upset every time a telemarketer calls can wreck your day. There is no need to get upset over something you can totally control. Why take it out on your family and guests?

Furthermore, why beat up the phone? I am sure you would rather spend your money other ways than of constantly replacing broken handsets!

5

Addictive Anger

Anger as soon as fed is dead. 'Tis starving makes it fat.

Emily Dickinson

As you are reading this, how would you respond to the following statements?

- I have a hard time living my life in moderation?
- I get bored quite easily and I always need something or someone to create excitement for me?
- I am the type of person who loves to take risks. I like to live on the edge!
- I get very depressed and suffer mood swings unless I am doing something stimulating.
- I love the intense rush that comes with getting angry!
- I sometimes get into fights, verbal or physical, because it gives me a sense of power and mastery over others.
- The adrenaline rush I get from my anger is better than any stimulating drug.
- Getting angry is better than sex!

If you answered yes to any of these statements or scored high in this section of the anger test, then you are likely to possess Addictive Anger.

As this type of anger implies, anger becomes very much like a substance abuse or "addiction" for the individual. Anger becomes a vice because it provides you with one or more of the following feelings:

- It gives a sense of instant gratification
- It provides relief to negative or depressive moods
- It offers some instant reward or reinforcement for the behavior

When I conduct seminars, workshops, support groups, and classes on anger-management, most individuals snicker or roll their eyes when they are taught about this type of anger. The most common question I am asked is, "Who in their right mind would want to get high or stoned on anger?"

That is a very fair question. I am going to give you three scenarios where you might see this type of anger used or precipitated.

☼

Scenario #1

There are some professional sports like boxing, football and hockey where fighting and aggression are expected and encouraged. Ever heard of the famous hockey expression: Last night I went to a fight and a hockey game broke out?

If you watch professional hockey, you are well aware each team carries one or two players referred to as "enforcers", "police officers" or "goons". Their chief role is to protect the higher skilled players on their teams by fighting with the "goons" from the other teams they play.

This type of player usually receives a minimal amount of ice time, but when they are called upon, they are out on the ice looking for a fight. They get pumped up on the bench as they await their "seek and destroy" mission!

Did you know this player is a catalyst for motivating their own team and fans? The fighting creates a frenzy and gets everyone including the fans pumped up! Everyone's adrenaline starts to rush.

Ask a minority of hockey fans and they will tell you they go to the games to see the fights. I have interviewed hockey fans in the past for other assignments and something really struck me. Many reported they welcomed the fights because they were very cathartic.

Catharsis means "release" or stress reducer. For these fans, watching two goons pounding it out on the ice was actually stress-relieving for them! In fact, some of these same fans said they sometimes wished they could suit up and get out there and toss a few punches!

What is the cause of anger? Boredom and the need for stimulation.

What are the precipitating factors? The need for a high level of arousal and adrenaline rush.

☼

Scenario #2

If you're a movie buff, you are probably familiar with the movie *Raging Bull*, which starred Robert DeNiro as Jake La Motta. It portrays the boxer both in and out of the ring.

As part of his pre-fight rituals, Jake orders his brother to slap him in the face and annoy him. Jake thrives on this aggression as a means for getting pumped up for his opponents. And guess what? It works!

In real life, you also see football players using aggression in the same way before and during the game. Their own teammates slap them around and yell at them to get them fire up.

Anger is used as a motivating factor!

What is the cause of anger? The perceived need for an external motivator.

What are the precipitating factors? Looking outside of yourself to satiate boredom, create excitement and fulfill some kind of longing for satisfaction.

☼

Scenario #3

For this example I will use the Friday night bruiser who likes going to bars to drink and then get into fights. Typically, this is an individual who lacks self-esteem, has come from an abusive family, has a history of being a bully, and believes the best form of communication involves some form of aggression.

Years ago I was working with individuals mandated into anger-management counseling because they were arrested for severe acts of aggression. What I found most disturbing is that these individuals had premeditated their Friday night fights. They purposely drank because they knew it would make them more aggressive.

In fact, I recall one individual telling me he would go to bars on the weekends when he knew they would be busy because he knew someone would bump into him and this would precipitate his anger and cause a fight.

When I asked him why would anyone want to get into a fight and possibly hurt someone, or even get hurt themselves, his simple response was, "The rush!"

What is the cause of anger? Loneliness and boredom.

What are the precipitating factors? The need for attention and recognition.

☼

Addictive anger for some becomes their vice. Part of my career involves working in the field of addictions both as a practitioner and as a professor. I find many individuals with addictions have extreme difficulty living their lives in moderation. Their lives are never in balance.

Over the years I have learned that some people really do possess "addictive" personalities. I believe they are socialized at an early age to become addictive by parents or someone close to them. They may have witnessed loved ones around them with addictions and have followed in their footsteps.

Have you ever heard the term "dry drunk"? This refers to an individual in recovery from alcoholism or another substance who then begins behaving obsessively or compulsively in some other form.

To them, rigorous attendance of support groups/counseling, or religious fundamentalism, is a substitute for their drinking or drugging. In essence, they have learned to control their substance abuse, but their addictive personality has not been modified.

Individuals with addictive anger are in some ways like "dry drunks". They are very addictive in their nature and need something external to stimulate their personalities. Much like a compulsive gambler who requires slot machines, card tables, roulette wheels, or bingos to provide them with an adrenaline rush, the addictive anger type requires aggressive conflict to satiate their thirst for adrenaline.

I have been told a number of times by individuals possessing this anger type that if they weren't getting into fights all the time, they would be as bored as hell! In fact, I have had some individuals actually tell me that if they weren't raging all the time, then they would have to find a stimulant such as cocaine, crack or ephedrine to provide them with this "superhuman" adrenaline rush they get.

Some time ago I asked Dr. William Glasser, the creator of *Reality Therapy*, for his view on addiction. He asserted something very profound. He believes *addiction separates you from people*.

People find happiness being around other people. On the other hand, the pleasure you find in addiction is usually solitary.

People with addictive anger need to find respectable social activities, events and means to satisfy their boredom.

6

Petrified Anger

*For every minute you remain angry, you give
up sixty seconds of peace of mind.*

Ralph Waldo Emerson

Here is a simple nature lesson to shed some light on petrified anger and its similarities to wood. Imagine, if you will, a healthy tree growing in the forest. It rests beside the water's edge. The tree is thriving and productive.

One day the tree becomes stressed with a disease, which persists for a prolonged period of time. Its ability to function weakens and insects, sensing this, start to feed on it until it eventually dies.

Over the years, the roots of the tree eventually rot out and the tree topples into the river. The fallen trunk and branches get swept away until it sinks to the bottom of the lake, where Mother Nature preserves the tree through petrifaction.

All things being equal, this tree will lie fixed in that state at the bottom of the lake for countless years. (Aquarium owners who have petrified drift wood in their aquariums can relate to what I am talking about!)

You are probably asking yourself: what does petrified driftwood have to do with anger? Simple! Anger follows the same kind of process petrified wood undergoes – over a period of time, behaviors, attitudes and personalities become solidified and preserved.

Imagine you are the tree. You function healthily and normally as a child. Everything seems to be good.

One day you are forced to deal with unwanted stresses and negativity. Someone does something bad to you or hurts you in a detrimental way. You perceive the event as very bad. You believe this situation has caused you prolonged or permanent harm.

The experience has left you feeling negative, cynical and hopeless. In fact, you feel sickened by the event or "diseased". You relive the event in your mind over and over, which further perpetuates the negative perception of what happened to you.

This only makes you angrier. This feeds your irrational thought process, eating away at you like a disease. Your thought process toward this event and similar ones becomes automatic.

Consequently, it becomes solidified or "petrified" like the tree at the bottom of the lake. Over a period of time you have formed a biased perception of what happened, and that becomes your "factual" truth.

Even if your perception of the event was wrong or those involved in causing you hurt tried to make amends, your petrified thought process distorts and shades your perception of the event.

Here are three examples of petrified anger at work:

☼

Scenario #1

Your best friend comes to you and tells you they are a little short of money that week for their bills. You offer to help them by giving them $50. They reluctantly accept the money, but only on the condition they will pay you back in full next month.

Being the decent, altruistic person you are, you say, "Not a problem, it's only fifty bucks, don't worry about it!"

Next month comes and your friend doesn't pay you back. It bothers you they never offered you the money, but you excuse it thinking they are short of money again and they will pay you when they get it.

Another couple of weeks pass. A month passes. Now you are really starting to get annoyed. Your friend has not once brought up the subject of the money they owe you. You are starting to feel used.

Finally, you start to drop hints to your friend. There is no response on their part. Unnerved, you come right out and ask about the money.

Your friend responds by telling you they were under the impression you didn't care about the money or expect to be paid back. This really sends you over the edge. How dare they take you and your money for granted!

Of course you can't just let bygones be bygones and swallow your pride. You take issue with your friend's complacency. Your friend tries to downplay the situation and even makes light of it, which further irritates you. You walk away angry.

They may or may not walk away angry as well, but they definitely know where they stand with you. The longer this situation lingers unresolved, the further apart the two of you grow.

Even if your friend repaid you the full amount with interest, this would still not be enough to salvage the friendship. The unpaid $50 is no longer the issue as it has become the principle of the matter. You want their most solemn, deepest part of the soul apology, which is never going to come.

Instead of forgiving and forgetting, you choose to hold onto the vendetta and wallow in the glory of knowing you were right and your friend was wrong. Basically, you feel it is better to be right and lose a friendship than be the one to cave in and accept your friend's apology.

In essence, you grow to enjoy reliving the bitter feelings you have toward your friend over and over.

What is the cause of your anger? Feeling used and taken for granted by your friend.

What are the precipitating factors? Not confronting your friend sooner and being honest with how you feel about them not paying you back.

You assumed they would pay you back even though you never asked them too. Are you madder at them or at yourself for not being more assertive in the first place?

☼

Scenario #2

Decades ago, your family and others were victims of war crimes. The wrongdoers have been brought to justice, some no longer living. You have never resolved the inner conflict and bitterness toward the race of people who committed these crimes.

Now when someone of that race tries to get friendly with you, you ignore them. You stereotype all people from that race as partaking in those war crimes. You feel it is most rewarding, perhaps vengeful to hate all people of that race or wish them ill wills.

You become what you've accused the perpetrators of the crimes and that race of people of being, racists!

What is the cause of your anger? Continued perceived wrongs done to you by others.

What are the precipitating factors? Your inability to forgive and let go of past transgressions that cannot be undone.

☼

Scenario #3

As a child your father left you, your siblings and your mother to support yourselves. For years you never heard a word from your father. You saw how your mother would cry herself to sleep nights. You saw how she was late with bill payments. You saw how she tried to contact him many times for some financial assistance and emotional support, but he never returned her calls. He wanted no part of any of you.

Now you are a young lady, you find it very difficult trusting men. In fact, a couple of the men you were last involved with elicited new trust issues. You pushed them away! You have a tendency to be distant with men because you worry about getting burned.

Your mantra is: "It is better to err on the side of caution than trust another man, especially after what your father did to you and your mother." No man will ever hurt me that way again!

According to you, "All men are the same!" Your belief system holds that all men are reasonable facsimiles of the father that deserted you. You have never overcome the hurts and disappointments he caused you.

Now you carry with you a hardened bitterness with which you flail every man you meet. You have chosen to hate all men!

What is the cause of your anger? Expecting men to be exactly the way you would like them to be and being disappointed when they are not.

What are the precipitating factors? Not forgiving your father for what he did to you and your family. Instead, you blame and accuse men you meet for being what your father was. You have made all men into psychological carbon copies of your father!

☼

For most individuals, petrified anger becomes second nature. When you ask them how long they have had this anger toward someone in particular, they can usually tell you in great details the times, dates and particulars of what happened.

People with petrified anger become obsessed with their feelings of anger and hostility. They derive a sense of satisfaction reliving what happened because it spurs feelings of rage. In their minds, they believe that by reliving the event, getting angry and feeling hatred toward the "wrongdoer" they exact some sort of revenge.

Nothing could be further from the truth. While you are reliving the event and getting yourself worked-up, the target of your hostility has more than likely moved on and could care less what happened. I am sure they felt some discomfort, hurt or anger in the beginning, but they have basically dumped it into the "out-of-sight-out-of-mind bin".

Wake up folks! These people are the ones who sleep well! While you're losing sleep still trying to flog a dead horse, these people are enjoying deep R.E.M. sleep.

Like resistant anger, people with petrified anger lock everything inside and cause themselves unnecessary suffering. If you keep reliving the same event over and over again, you are like an individual suffering posttraumatic stress disorder (PTSD).

PTSD carries with it some very unpleasant feelings and physical disorders:

- Bitterness
- Flashbacks
- Depression
- Anxiety
- Fear
- Nausea/vomiting
- Insomnia
- Constant worrying
- Irritability
- Increased alcohol/drug consumption
- Bodily aches and pains
- Increased blood pressure
- Increased heart rate

In essence, petrified anger is a mocked form of PTSD. The individual truly believes they were victimized, abused or exploited.

For some, their distorted reality leads them to believe they were a "casualty of war", much like an individual who suffers PTSD from serving in the Vietnam or the Persian Gulf War.

What many individuals don't understand is that by reliving their experiences repetitiously, the mind tricks the body into believing the experience is real. The body reacts accordingly and prepares itself for fight mode.

Over a period of time, you actually tax your body by putting it into what Walter Cannon called the "Fight or Flight Syndrome", where you keep creating adrenaline rushes that tax the central nervous system. Given time, the body could actually suffer from what Hans Selye found in his "General Adaptation Syndrome" model.

In a very condensed form, this model asserts that the more we dwell in this "high state of alertness" the more we drain ourselves and weaken our immune systems, possibly causing serious or permanent damage.

The best way to summarize how this model fits in with petrified anger is as follows, from top down:

Event
Anger
Bitterness
Relive Experience
Elevated Blood Pressure
Adrenaline Rush
Repeat Cycle Too Many Times
Weakened Immune System
Exhaustion (mental or physical illness)

Is it really worth feeling this bitterness toward someone? Does it really bring you so much satisfaction that you're prepared to age faster and become sick? Is your life like the TV show, *The Sopranos*, or like the movie *The Godfather* or *Good Fellas*, where vendettas are the only way to settle old scores?

Always remember, forgiveness goes along way for everyone involved, mostly you!

7

Compressive Anger

People who fly into a rage always make a bad landing.

Will Rogers

If you possess this type of anger you are a walking time-bomb!

Three things to know right from the word go:

1. You possess a short fuse
2. You have a sensitive trigger, and
3. Others close to you probably know which buttons to push to get you going

Earlier in the book I discussed that anger is a normal, healthy emotion that everyone experiences. I also alluded to the point that individuals who "act crazy" when they are angry give anger its negative, maniacal connotation. This is compressive anger.

I've had clients, colleagues and friends claiming they go from zero to sixty in 0.001 seconds when they snap! In fact, when I ask them what they are thinking about to get themselves in this dither, they claim they didn't have time to think. They just explode!

Of course, this is not true. You have to think about something first before you can create that feeling for yourself. I will, however, assert there are certain individuals out there who are puppeteers who know exactly what buttons to go after to stimulate you to explode faster if you possess this type of anger.

The following are three scenarios that depict compressive anger. All possess the same element, becoming irrational without first rationalizing.

☼

<u>Scenario #1</u>

You are rushing for work. You've waited until the last minute to get things done. What you could have prepared the night before you've put off until the morning. Unforeseen obstacles arise, as they usually do, and your kids are not co-operating with you. You ask yourself, "Why me?"

This further fuels your fire. You start to believe everyone is against you. There are some mysterious forces at work trying to make you miserable. You thrive on this irrational belief process and this precipitates greater frustration.

Finally, the kids are off to school and you are on your way to work. If traffic is co-operative, you will make it to work with 30 seconds to a minute to spare. It looks good. You're going to do it! That was until the train came, the long one.

Guess what? You're going to be late for work! You sit and stew in the car, pounding the steering wheel and cursing at the top of your lungs at the engineer.

What is the cause of your anger? Frustration.

What are the precipitating factors for your anger? Bad planning, procrastination.

☼

Scenario #2

You come home from work. Your teenage son has 4 pairs of shoes strewn about the hallway. He is sitting in the living room with his feet propped up on the coffee table. This in itself is enough to ignite your ire.

However, there are bigger fish to fry. The night before, you had asked him to cut the lawn. In fact it was more of an order you barked, seeing as he didn't cut the lawn the three previous days when asked. You confront him and ask him why the lawn isn't cut, as if you really need an answer. From the time you pulled into the driveway until you saw him seated on the sofa, you couldn't wait to confront him.

You didn't have such a great day at work today. It was a matter of time before your fuse was fully lit. Before he even has a chance to give you a reason, you tear into him. Your blood is boiling and the foulest of words start spewing from your mouth.

You feel your head getting lighter and hot. Your temple starts beating at a feverish rate. You've gone from zero to sixty in microseconds.

This sets the tempo for the rest of your evening as you start yelling at other members of your family. At night's end, you go to bed with a migraine headache and no one wants to talk to you. And one more thing… the lawn never did get cut!

What is the cause of your anger? Stress, frustration and disappointment.

What are the precipitating factors for your anger? Lack of discipline and lack of corrective consequences.

☼

Scenario #3

Heather arrives home from work late. Her husband Anthony inquires as to why she is late. She informs him that she stopped for coffee with some of her girlfriends after work to plan for an upcoming baby shower.

Anthony is irate she would do that and not come home and have dinner ready for the kids. Anthony starts yelling and demanding that her place is in the home to support her family. Anthony accuses her of not caring for the kids or him. He asserts she does this on purpose to defy him.

In the past he has had a history of abusing Heather both verbally and physically. Recently, he reluctantly agreed to her working again after she threatened to leave him. Anthony believes she is "taking advantage" of her freedom. Before they discuss the situation any further, Anthony is already grabbing her arm!

What is the cause of anger? Anthony's irrational beliefs.

What are the precipitating factors? Lack of communication, unrealistic expectations, irrational and rigid thinking.

☼

Compressive anger is perhaps one of the most serious anger types as it has the propensity to cause immediate harm.

The hallmark of compressive anger is the *loss of ability* to rationalize and control the situation. In fact, this type of anger usually causes the individual to lose control of themselves as well as the situation.

The key ingredients in this anger are violence and aggression, two emotions that eventually lead to irreparable damage.

Over the years, I have worked with many clients and couples who possessed this type of anger. This type of anger is very common in domestic violence and Battered Spouse Syndrome.

I believe all forms of violence are wrong and should not be tolerated. No one should stay in abusive relationships as they are not only harmful to the victim, but to the children who witness this abuse as well.

Typically, domestic abusers possess compressive anger and their spouse usually becomes the target of their projected low self-esteem and inadequacies. More often than not, abusers come from abusive dysfunctional families themselves. They were either a victim of abuse or watched one parent abuse the other. They irrationally learned that aggression solves problems, which is furthest from the truth.

In my book *Why Women Want What They Can't Have*, I discuss why people stay in abusive relationships and the dynamics involved. The book focuses on Object Relations Cycle and the whole gambit of abuse.

To quickly summarize the abuse, in many cases men tend to use physical abuse and women use emotional abuse, or push their partner's buttons to antagonize the abuse.

This may sound ludicrous, and I am in no way saying abused women seek abuse or ask for it, but many become patterned participators in the cycle of abuse. They realize their partners are bigger and stronger and the only damage they can do to retaliate is emotionally (aggravate/abuse).

In most domestic abuse situations the cycle plays like a broken record, which follows the same repetitious script. She knows he has a short fuse and intentionally or unintentionally provokes him to eruption. Once he becomes abusive, she mocks him and points out, "See, you never changed, you still pick on women." Or, "Wow, it takes a lot of courage to beat on a helpless woman."

This is further likely to frustrate his already weakened ego state and perpetuate additional violence.

I spoke with Dr. Susan Weitzman, author of *Not To People Like Us!* which focuses on domestic abuse in upper-class families. She told me something that reaffirmed my own findings: Men can become habituated to abusing their wives, while their wives can become habituated to certain lifestyles and use excuses to justify the abuse.

People with compressive anger need to take anger-management counseling, workshops, or support groups in order to identify their triggers and nip "trigger manipulation" in the bud. Most people with compressive anger commonly identify certain people or situations in their lives as their triggers.

Unfortunately, most will blame the situation or the person rather than identifying their own interpretation and irrational belief system as the core problem.

Once you can identify what your triggers are, then you can interpret your irrational thinking patterns. The key is to learn to respond differently to the people or situations that you believe provoke you.

If you recall, most people with compressive anger problems will assert their anger happens too fast, from zero to sixty in microseconds! They contend they don't have time to think, they just explode!

Quite the opposite is true. You do have time to think, as it is your perception of the situation first, then your irrational thinking process (albeit fast) that leads you to feeling anger. I believe some individuals learn this anger like a skill or talent through repetition and are capable of putting minimal mental effort to get them to that level of anger.

Stereotypes are short-cuts to perceptions. Moreover, they are lazy perceptions. Rather than look at each situation and individual differently each time, you start to stereotype similar situations you're in or individuals you see often. You expect them to be the same and behave the same, thus stimulating your preconceived notions for how you will respond.

In abusive relationships, both parties play out the anger and abuse as if they were reciting the same script over and over again. In fact, many of my former clients would say it started the same way, the plot was the same and the outcome was predictable.

People can master their compressive anger much like a musician masters the piano, a golfer perfects their swing or smoker lights a cigarette! It becomes second nature with minimal thought invested.

8

Jealousy

*Anger and jealousy can no more bear to lose
sight of their objects than love.*

George Eliot

Besides being one of the seven deadly sins, jealousy is also a type of anger some people possess. When left unchecked and allowed to progress, jealousy can escalate into other anger types, such as petrified and compressive.

Individuals with jealousy anger develop it through repeated experiences of rejection, betrayal and loss. Many of their experiences occurred very early in life when they experienced some kind of abandonment/rejection from a parent, or they experience personal loss, perhaps the death of a loved one.

Some individuals may have been raised in a lower class environment where nice clothing, shoes, toys and opportunities were hard to come by and other children who were more fortunate, made fun of them and belittled them. This could have led to rejection by their peers, or made them feel unwanted and worthless.

The hallmark of jealousy anger is *perceived ownership* and possession. The individual with jealousy has learned to try to possess whatever comes into their life.

Many individuals who have jealousy issues usually live their lives in fear of rejection or loss. The pain of losing someone or being rejected early on in life created deep wounds that never healed. Individuals are also likely to have never forgiven those who have wronged them in the past and this has only caused the wound of jealousy to fester deeper.

These are some of the negative attributes associated with jealousy:

- Angered by people more successful than you.
- Believes the world owes you something.
- Believes there is some higher power in control who manipulates people like puppets on a string.
- Believes loyalty exists to one person only.
- Always believes in reciprocity when you do something for another person.
- Needs to be the focal point of attention from partners and best friends.
- Keeps a running score card of favors done for others.
- Possesses irrational beliefs where you believe people are conspiring to hurt you or use you.
- Fears getting close to others due to fear of rejection.
- Possessiveness of loved ones or things you own.
- Fears commitment.
- Checking and stalking behaviors of those you are currently involved with or former relationships.
- Uses abusive and controlling behaviors.

☼

There is a psychological term listed in the fourth edition of the *Diagnostic and Statistical Manual of Mental Disorders*

(DSM-IV) called Obsessive Compulsive Personality Disorder (OCPD). People with the disorder obsess over thoughts, which create stress and frustration. They may also engage in obsessing behaviors such as checking, washing, locking etc. to alleviate their tensions.

This by no means is a form of jealousy anger. I have counseled clients possessing OCPD, the hallmarks of which include: perfectionism, controlling behaviors, possession and irrational jealousy. In most cases, individuals did in fact experience rejection and loss early on life, along with other factors which led to them developing this disorder.

Moreover, people with this disorder usually possessed jealousy anger!

Here are some examples that illustrate jealousy anger:

☼

Scenario #1

Ten year old Allan gets reprimanded by his fifth grade school teacher for punching a classmate who had taken the atlas from Allan's desk.

The atlas belongs to the classroom and Allan had used the book to find some destinations for a class project on which he was working. He was finished with the book, but left it on his desk. The student asked Allan if he could use the atlas and Allan said no.

Observing Allan away from the desk, working on something else, the student thought he would quickly look up something and return the book to the desk before Allan noticed.

When sent to the principal's office, it was acknowledged that Allan had a history of stealing small articles from other students as well as hoarding.

What is the cause of Allan's anger? Jealousy.

What are the precipitating factors? Feeling inadequate, low self-esteem, feeling the need for power.

☼

<u>Scenario #2</u>

After repeated marital counseling and interventions, Lucy has finally decided to leave her husband Tim. After four years of marriage, the two biggest complaints Lucy has about Tim is his refusal to share his feelings with her and that there is little, if any, communication in their marriage.

Lucy has voiced her need for emotional intimacy repeatedly, but Tim has told her that it's "not him" and he is not into "that pop-psychology crap". Frustrated, Lucy has made the decision to move on with her life.

Acknowledging the severity of the situation, Tim has agreed to marital counseling. Lucy has told him it is too late for that! Tim tells her he will do whatever it takes to save their marriage and promises to change.

Lucy points out that this has been a common element of manipulation throughout their four years, that whenever she threatens to leave he promises to change. Unfortunately, the "changes" last long enough to appease her, and for him to become complacent again. After repeated attempts to salvage the marriage, Tim realizes she is gone for good his time.

But now a year has passed and Tim is still stalking her! Lucy started dating someone only to see the relationship fail because he was afraid of the threats Tim was making. Tim keeps telling her he has changed and to "Please give me one last chance!"

What is the cause of Tim's anger? Rejection, feeling abandoned, feeling betrayed.

What are the precipitating factors? Perhaps rejection in childhood from parents, loved ones or repeated failed relationships with women he has been intimate with in the past.

☼

Scenario #3

Marty works at a blue-collar job and pulls in an average income. He is married with two children. They live next door to the Johnson's. Mr. Johnson is professionally employed and "only buys the best" for his family. The Johnson kids are always bragging to Marty's kids about what their parents bought them.

Marty's own wife and children have sarcastically said they wished they had more, or were rich. Deep down, this really bothers Marty. He wishes he could offer them more, but the opportunity to earn a higher income is just not possible.

Worse, most of his income goes toward the mortgage, bills and "keeping up with the Johnsons". Marty's wife has not worked in four years since their daughter was born. She believes the man should be the bread winner in the family and refuses to go back to work. She believes it is Marty's duty to provide a lifestyle comparable to the Johnson family.

On several occasions, Marty has suggested they move into a more modest house that would allow them to get out of debt faster. His wife does not agree. Mr. Johnson has just purchased a top of the line car.

At the dinner table that night, his wife starts asking when they will buy a new car. Frustrated and fed up, Marty leaves the table and takes off for a few hours, drinking at a local bar.

Arriving home close to midnight, he ogles the new car in the Johnson driveway. He notices all the lights are off in their house. He picks up a rock from his flowerbed and throws it at the car. He hits it dead on and the alarm sounds. He disappears into the house just as the lights in the Johnson house flash on.

What is the cause of Marty's anger? Envy and jealousy.

What are the precipitating factors? Financial stress, emotional stress and frustration.

☼

Individuals with jealousy anger type feel inadequate about themselves much of the time. They compare themselves to others they wish they were like, or yearn for what others have.

Interestingly, they often deny ever wanting to be like anyone else. In fact, they criticize those they most want to be like – their success, their possessions, their money – critical of anything positive or beautiful about them.

Some people with jealousy anger are also likely to use putdowns in front of people to try and make themselves look better.

Perhaps the worst place to see jealousy anger rearing its ugly head is after the breakup of a relationship. When the individual with jealousy gets rejected and feels spurned, they will go to great lengths to try and salvage the relationship. It is during this time the individual will try to bargain, compromise and promise to change in order to be given one more chance.

When the final dissolution of the marriage becomes obvious to the "rejected", they are unwilling to accept the outcome. They believe that if they "could just get their ex-mate to listen and give them another chance", things would work out. They begin pressuring their ex-mate for "another chance", further pushing them away.

As their ex-mate pulls further away, however, they start to pursue them, believing persistence produces romance. What they believe to be romantic often times becomes stalking behaviors, harassment and aggression. This only alienates their estranged spouse more, causing fear and resentment.

When you examine domestic cases where "peace bonds" or restraining orders have been issued, the perpetrator usually possesses jealousy anger.

Individuals with jealousy anger really do need counseling, support groups or courses that will enhance self-esteem building. Moreover, those with unresolved issues stemming from childhood probably require more intense therapy to reprogram their tendency to irrational thinking.

9

Road Rage

In times of great stress or adversity, it's always best to keep busy, to plow your anger and your energy into something positive.

Lee Iacocca

Over the last decade or so, much has been made about road rage. I have been asked by police, why I think the number of road rage incidents has increased and continues to increase?

I believe there are a number of reasons we are seeing the number of enraged drivers losing it on road ways:

- Increases in the number of drivers
- City populations are growing
- People are becoming lazy drivers, in that they take for granted the rules of the road and don't signal
- Lack of courtesy to other drivers
- We live in an instant gratification society where we are always rushing
- Bad time-management leading to lateness/rushing
- Influx of immigrants who abide according to their own cultural driving norms
- Multi-tasking while driving: talking on the phone, texting, smoking, eating/drinking, watching television,

reading the paper, putting on make-up, shaving, arguing with children
- A greater number of larger/taller vehicles around that you can't see over: SUV's, pick-up trucks and vans
- Lack of law enforcement for traffic violators
- Too many places to get too in a short period of time
- Simply put, just bad drivers

☼

The most common complaint I usually hear is that the age of the driver is the reason road rage occurs. Notice I didn't list this above? I don't believe the age of the driver has anything to do with road rage. I often hear young drivers complaining about seniors driving too slow or erratically. On the other hand, I hear elder drivers complain that younger drivers drive too fast or too recklessly!

I also hear women complain about men driving without any courtesy or sensitivity. Conversely, I hear men complain about female drivers multi-tasking, which causes erratic driving. I have also heard that it's only members of a certain culture or country that are the worst drivers, which I also don't buy!

There are a number of reasons that lead to poor driving and eventually to road rage. After speaking with individuals in law enforcement, particularly highway and traffic divisions, I've compiled a list of traffic infractions that can lead to road rage or are episodes of road rage.

Do you:

- Follow too closely vehicles in front of you?

- Fail to signal when changing lanes?
- Drive too fast, way above the speed limit?
- Flash your high beams at slow drivers in front of you?
- Cut people off intentionally?
- Purposely go too slow or keep braking to annoy drivers behind you?
- Purposely speed up to prevent other cars from passing?
- Run amber and red lights?
- Ignore the flashing lights/stop signs of school buses?
- Fail to pull over when an EMS vehicle has its lights flashing?
- Drive too slow in the fast/passing lane on the highway?
- Make obscene gestures or yell at other drivers?
- Throw your trash/litter out the window?
- Multi-task instead of paying attention to the road when driving?
- Drive an unsafe vehicle, or vehicle that pollutes the air?
- Drive without a seat belt?
- Drive recklessly on purpose to impress passengers?
- Engage in races with other drivers while putting others at risk?
- Drive while intoxicated or too tired?
- Follow drivers who have wronged you to try and even the score, or confront them by arguing or fighting?
- Throw objects or spit at other vehicles?
- Chase after someone while calling the police to report them?
- Threaten other drivers with a weapon?

- Follow another driver home or to a parking lot and cause damage to their vehicle while they are way from it?
- Purchase a larger vehicle with the sole purpose of intimidating other drivers?

If you answered yes to several of these questions, then you might consider yourself a "road rager"!

Some individuals I interviewed report becoming a whole different personality when they get behind the wheel of their car. In fact, some have told me they feel more powerful and indestructible. They crank up the volume on the radio and they feel ready to conquer the Indy 500!

Also, I have had some drivers tell me they feel a certain anonymity or disassociation from themselves when they climb into their vehicles. This is very true for those who have tinted or blackened windows where you can't see into their vehicles.

Some drivers reported "feeling trapped" as their prime catalysts. They find being caught in traffic jams intolerable, which makes them feel uncomfortable. Many times, when people are already late for appointments, bumper to bumper traffic only adds to their frustration, which may spill out as aggression.

Drivers operating smaller cars often complain about larger vehicles and trucks when they are stuck in traffic. Many say the most annoying aspect of their experience is their inability to see around the large vehicle in front of them.

Others complain about the inability to see around a large vehicle engaged in stop and go traffic, which becomes tedious due to the sudden stops. This experience sends individuals into irate states, some actually challenging transport trucks in their little sedans!

Here are three examples of road rage in action. Perhaps you can relate to one or all of them?

☼

Scenario #1

You are driving in the fast lane of the highway in route to your cottage, usually a four-hour trip. The trip starts out well until you hit the main arteries of the highway where traffic gets congested. This will easily delay your arrival time by at least an hour. Your kids in the back seat start complaining that they are bored. "Are we there yet?" starts up.

This gets under your skin, especially listening to your wife repetitively sighing and telling them to shut up. Finally, there is a bit of a break in the traffic. You put the foot to the metal and try to make up for lost time. It looks clear in front of you, but you worry this might not last long, that there might be further congestion down the road, so you go even faster.

Your wife warns you about your speed and you tell her to mind her own business. Fifteen minutes later, a highway ranger tags you for speeding. You were caught doing way above the maximum speed.

You are even more upset with the highway ranger for being unsympathetic to your cause. You flunk the attitude test and he charges you to the maximum!

What is the cause of your anger? Road rage caused by stress and frustration.

What are the precipitating factors? Feeling righteously justified to speed because the traffic jam has inconvenienced your vacation.

☼

Scenario #2

It's holiday season and you wait until the last minute to do your gift buying. Not feeling at all in the holiday spirit, you force yourself to the shopping mall. Just trying to find a parking place is impossible. Finally, you see a car pulling out and you race to the spot.

You arrive at exactly the same moment as another driver. You both position your cars toward the spot so neither one of you can get in. You honk at one another and make obscene gestures. Cars are starting to line up as they try to pass. These drivers are now getting upset. You won't budge, neither will the other driver.

Eventually, the mall security comes and asks both of you to get out of your cars. You both reluctantly agree. Security asks one of you to find another spot. Neither of you will agree to this. There is no way you will give up "your" coveted spot!

After ten more minutes of this absurd behavior, a police officer arrives at the scene. You are both informed neither will get the spot. This makes you totally irate and you start complaining to the police officer. You start yelling at the other driver and making threats.

Before you know it, you are being charged with uttering threats, disturbing the peace and obstructing justice! All in the name of a parking spot.

What is the cause of your anger? Believing that another driver showed no respect for you.

What are the precipitating factors? Feeling cheated/robbed of the spot, frustrated by the traffic in the parking lot and believing others didn't respect your value as a human being.

☼

Scenario #3

You are driving on the highway and it seems everyone is doing at least ten miles an hour over the speed limit. The highway is three lanes wide and you keep pace with the flow. You are on your way to work, which normally takes a half hour, but you think you can shave ten minutes off your arrival time.

A sports car flies past you as do two others. You decide to keep pace with them and begin following behind. Easily, they are twenty miles an hour over the speed limit. There are at least five cars now in front of you as you trail behind.

Suddenly, out of nowhere you see sirens flashing behind you. You pull into the right hand lane expecting the cop to drive past you and ticket one of the sports cars. As you move into the right lane, so does the cop. It is you who gets ticketed!

You start yelling at the cop for pulling you over. "How come those cars going a lot faster weren't caught first?" The cop says nothing other than you were going well over the speed limit and breaking the law and you are the one getting the ticket.

After all is said and done, you get back into your car and onto the highway, purposely driving the speed limit in the fast lane and forcing traffic to pass you.

What is the cause of your anger? Believing you were wrongly ticketed and mistreated.

What are the precipitating factors? Irrationally believing that if other people break the law then it must be okay and that you are no longer accountable. Minimizing the wrong you were doing and maximizing the same wrong others were doing.

☼

With all the technological advances and safety features in motor vehicles, traffic fatalities are not diminishing. In fact, it seems that the rates of driving violations keep increasing.

One of the greatest concerns I have observed, as have many traffic enforcement officials, is the growing number of people running not just amber, but red lights too! I have interviewed people I know who run amber lights and asked them why? Their responses are startling.

Some asserted that they had been hit from behind in the past because they were slowing down to stop for an amber light. The driver behind had expected them to run the amber light so they didn't even try to slow down. The next thing they knew, the driver behind them was glued to their bumper!

Some people have consciously or unconsciously set their minds to this apprehension and hold no qualms about running the light. A colleague and friend of mine who is a cop made an interesting observation. When pulling over drivers who had run amber and red lights, he got these responses.

Red light violators said, "I'm sorry, I know I did wrong by running that light! Please go easy on me." Conversely, amber light violators most often reported the following, "It was only yellow and thought I could beat it before it turned red!" Yellow means stop too at traffic lights!

I predict in the near future, there will be more defensive driving classes, driving skills classes and stiffer penalties for road rage offenders. If fatalities continue to increase and insurance premiums go up, society will have no choice other than to re-educate people to improve their driving skills.

10

Conflictual Anger

Anger is never without an argument, but seldom with a good one.

George Saville

Would you consider yourself to be an over-analytical person? Are you always beating things to death until you get the answer you want? Most times are you still not satisfied with the answer?

Has anyone ever referred to you as a fault finder? Are you able to find the black cloud in the rainbow? Do you make mountains out of mole hills? Do you enjoy getting into arguments and disagreements with others because this gives you a sense of power and control?

If you answered yes to one or more of these statements then you might be an individual who possesses conflictual anger!

The trademark of this type of anger is feeling a sense of inferiority. Psychoanalyst Alfred Adler referred to individuals who have low self-esteem, lack communication skills and possess poor social skills as being those most likely to possess this complex. Generally, people feeling outcast from society are likely to feel inferior.

This complex was created early in life when they were rejected by their parents, families, were part of dysfunctional families, or felt rejected by society. They felt they did not fit in and started to develop feelings of alienation and even isolation.

Many people who go through this process become extremely passive and may even become depressed. Some develop a sense of learned helplessness and this facilitates the onset of depression and hopelessness.

Some individuals with inferiority complexes grow frustrated and discontent with their current situations. Rather than remain in a helpless and hopeless mindset, they learn to overcome these passive feelings by replacing them with more aggressive feelings. These aggressive feelings create an altogether new complex known as the superiority complex.

Individuals learn how to overcome their sense of helplessness and rejection by developing a more aggressive thinking style. They become fed-up with the fact they were rejected early on in life. They despise further rejection!

Instead of feeling victimized, they learn to be the "rejecters". If they reject others first, before they get rejected, then they no longer feel helpless and worthless.

Some learned to "even up the score" by being a bully. They abuse or reject others first before it can be done to them.

Of course, many of these individuals actually misperceived others' intentions. Others could have been intending the best, but because of repeated rejection the one being rejected perceives all situations as the same!

The key element in this type of anger is a sense of *feeling powerful* through the creation of arguments, conflicts and disagreements.

The individual possesses some degree of a superiority complex because of their previous/present feelings of inferiority and they engage others in arguments as a means of flexing their superiority.

I have had colleagues in the world of law enforcement assert that some individuals wish to become cops because it would give them a sense of power and authority they have never felt. They would be able to use their badge as an extension of their manhood. One police officer I know has referred to this as "little, big man syndrome".

I have even heard stories from others who wear shirts one size too small to make them appear larger, or wear shirts one or two sizes bigger so the label on the shirt makes them appear larger than they are!

Here are some examples that demonstrate how individuals display conflictual anger. Perhaps you can see some of these traits in yourself?

☼

Scenario #1

As a member of the school board you are expected to regularly attend staff meetings. After the last meeting, the principal of the school called you into his office to discuss some concerns. Some teachers have accused you of harboring hidden agendas and purposely creating arguments and disagreements, even over the smallest of issues.

For years, you have felt that no one really listens to you. And when you do make your point known, no one takes you seriously. You find others, especially at staff meetings, are always getting their stupid suggestions validated by other teachers. Lately, since challenging their suggestions, it seems your colleagues now find you to be argumentative.

In closing your meeting with the principle, he points out that from his own observations you are probably alienating your colleagues and they are probably going to pull further way from you.

What is the cause of your anger? Feeling inferior to your peers.

What are the precipitating factors? Believing your peers think they are better than you. Holding the perception that, if the former statement is true, this makes you worthless.

☼

Scenario #2

You write letters to your local newspaper on a weekly basis. Everyone in your community knows who you are. Unfortunately, you are getting known as a "fault finder". It seems all your letters come across as attacks on members in political offices and government expenditures.

Over the last year, you have applied for several jobs and no one is calling you in for interviews. In fact, some of the positions for which you applied were being advertised by the same government officials you had lambasted in the newspapers.

You call the places to which you have applied, to inquire as to how you might qualify for a job, but they do not return your phone calls. This makes you more irate and you criticize the city even further in your new letters.

What is the cause of your anger? Being rejected. This inflames your elevated sense of self-worth.

What are the precipitating factors? Frustration over being rejected, yet this was self-created.

☼

Scenario #3

Before going to work, you and your wife had an argument over the smallest of things. In fact, your wife tells you she can't even remember how the argument even started. You remember though! Before leaving the house, you still take another jab at getting in the last word.

As you arrive home, you see her car parked in the driveway. You are fuming over the fact that she never called you at work to say hi. You begin telling yourself she believes you were wrong and that she was right, thus winning the argument.

You grow more furious! You are already planning for the argument you will start once you get in the house. You drive around the block a couple of times just to make sure you have the argument and rebuttal fine-tuned!

What is the cause of your anger? A sense of self-righteousness and the fear of being wrong.

What are the precipitating factors? Perhaps repeated failures in the past, feeling worthless and believing that mistakes imply not only failing in that situation but also failing as a person.

☼

Conflictual anger has its roots in failures experienced early on in life, which were either magnified by parents, teachers or caregivers.

You internalized the failure as being *representative of you* as a person. You may have learned from parental disputes that solutions arise from fighting, albeit they were dysfunctional most times. You were taught to believe that being abrasive or argumentative produces results.

Ever heard the expression, "The squeaky wheel always gets the oil"? For this type of anger, I am not just referring to a squeaky wheel, rather the entire rusting axel!

Let me ask you a question: Is it better to be wrong and still have friends and people like you, or is it better to be right and win arguments with the risk of alienating people?

Most people with conflictual anger fall into the second part of the question. They trick themselves into believing they would admit their mistakes when they are wrong. What feeds their anger is their inability to accept and believe they could be wrong!

To accept being wrong would mean they are bad people who make stupid decisions. If this is the case, then this must make them stupid people!

Although this line of logic may sound ridiculous, this has become the thinking process for the individual with conflictual anger. They need to stop being overly critical of themselves and with perception that others are always judging their performances.

If an actor were to play a role in a movie that absolutely stank, would this make them a bad actor? Definitely not. It was only a single event. In reality, this shouldn't make or break the person.

Furthermore, if the actor's performances in all of the movies they appeared in stank, would this make them a bad person overall? Definitely not! You have to *separate the person from their performance*.

There is no such thing as a bad person. There are people who do bad things. Individuals with conflictual anger need to distinguish between these two states and remove the "perfectionist" pressures they are placing on themselves and others.

Remember, discussions can be just discussions. They do not always have to become arguments!

11

Habitual Anger

*Resentment is like taking poison and waiting
for the other person to die.*

Malachy McCourt

Has anyone close to you ever told you that you seem angry most of the time? Perhaps all of the time?

Do you feel angry most of the day every day? Do you tend to watch a lot of movies that have vengeance, aggression and violence as their central theme? Does this act as a catharsis for you, helping you relieve your own feelings of aggression? Do you tend to have recurrent or similar dreams that have anger and violence? Do you seem to wake up angry each day and go to bed each night feeling angry?

You might not know it, but these are some of the most common attributes of those possessing habitual anger!

As its name implies, habitual anger is a habit, and it is no different from making happiness, joy and peace your preferred feelings. Anger is a choice!

This type of anger usually started early in life. It persisted into teenage years because of repetition. It eventually stuck because the candidate possessing this type of anger never challenged themselves to acknowledge or change it.

Habitual anger may have become a conditioned response to witnessing parents and caregivers who were angry most of the time. You might have grown up in a very depressed environment where dysfunction was the norm.

Having repeatedly experienced this type of negativity and pessimism, it could have led you to ongoing frustrations. Ultimately, this culminated in you becoming an angry person.

Habitual anger is very easy to see in others when you are on the outside looking in. If you are on the inside looking out, when others point your anger out to you, it only infuriates you. Like pouring gasoline on a fire, your habitual anger consumes you that much more!

Here are some examples where habitual anger is most often seen. If you possess habitual anger, do you see yourself in any of these situations?

☼

Scenario #1

You got to bed late last night. You were tired, but couldn't sleep. It could have been drinking the two cups of coffee close to bed time. You tossed and turned most of the night. Finally, just when you fell asleep, you were rudely awakened by your blaring clock radio. Worse, the song that woke you is one you absolutely despise!

It's time to get up and get ready for work. You rush to put out your garbage that you should have put out the night before. As you dump the garbage bin at the street, your smiling friendly neighbor wishes you a good morning. Seeing your neighbor all bright and cheery annoys you even more.

You get in the car and drive to work. Everyone is either driving too slow or too fast. You believe some drivers are purposely making you late for work. Every radio station is playing the same "garbage" music, or the damn disk jockeys are all talking blather!

You smile at another co-worker as you pull into the parking lot but they fail to return a smile. This infuriates you. You hold the door open for some people on the way in and there is not so much as a "thank you". You tell yourself people are annoying. You hate them!

What is the cause of your anger? Entitlement. Believing life owes you more and that things should be easier.

What are the precipitating factors? Stress and frustration caused by negative perceptions and expectations of others.

☼

Scenario #2

You get the newspaper first thing in the morning and read the headlines. Every headline is screaming doom and gloom. You read about what the government is doing and what it isn't doing. This infuriates you.

You decide to save time getting ready for work so you turn on the television to get more informed about what is going on in the world. It seems three out of every four news captions are either discussing wars, acts of terrorism or problems with the economy. The world is full of nothing but chaos and disarray!

You start to think about the dead-end job to which you are going out of necessity in order to pay your bills and ask yourself, "What's the point? The government just taxes me to death anyway."

It seems everything in life is a waste of time! No matter how hard you try to get ahead you get screwed! The news reaffirms your negative beliefs about people and the world. Your day is wrecked before you've even left the house.

What is the cause of your anger? Seeking out negative affirmations, which reinforce your negative expectations of people and the world.

What are the precipitating factors? Maintaining negative stereotypes and attraction to negativity. Like attracts like! Your negative outlook is a magnet that attracts and seeks out like-minded themes.

☼

Scenario #3

You hate the way people drive. It makes you angry that bad things are always happening to innocent people. You hate paying taxes. You believe the government is a bunch of crooks.

Waiting in lines at grocery stores or gas pumps annoys you. It annoys you when delivery people don't deliver things on time. Your neighbor's garbage blew onto your lawn, you could kill him! Your satellite receiver went down, and man you're miffed!

The damn weather! It rains or snows all the time. People stare at you in restaurants when you are eating. How dare they? And if that isn't enough, your food is always overcooked or cold. You go to have a bath and there's not enough hot water. Damn the kids outside having fun and screaming! They are so annoying.

Your flight has been delayed due to inclement weather. Damn pilot! No one co-operates with you. Everyone is against you.

What is the cause of your anger? Being a fault finder and expecting everything to be the way you like it.

What are the precipitating factors? Setting yourself and others up to fail or fall short of the mark. You personalize situations and really believe the world hates you and you are always angry. Expect the worst and hope for the best!

☼

Habitual anger has as its core the *unwillingness to change* the negative, faulty thinking style. Those with habitual anger believe they are right to be angry all the time because in many ways they really believe people are purposely out to make them miserable.

The greatest challenge of the individual with habitual anger is to try and change their irrational thinking. They never hope for the best, and always expect the worst. They are pessimistic thinkers who believe that by being guarded in their emotions (i.e. being cynical all the time) they minimize the risk of being disappointed.

Habituated thinkers are lazy thinkers! They never challenge preconceived notions and irrational beliefs. They take whatever they are given and go with it even though their perceptions are totally misplaced. They are the bearers of doom and gloom.

Remember, stereotypes are shortcuts to perceptions. When you use stereotypes to think, you are acting as a passive thinker. You are not challenging your thought process to see other reasons, options or outcomes. You are most likely to interpret similar situations the same way. In fact, you may even start using the same reaction for all situations – angry thinking!

In Scenario #3, I mentioned things with which people become angry; bad weather, waiting in lines, technical inconveniences and other unfortunate situations. Do you get angry when these things happen to you?

If yes, then I have this next question for you: How does getting angry possibly help, improve or change the situation?

Getting angry over things out of your control only frustrates you and always makes things worse.

Habituated anger in many ways is like an addiction. This type of anger has already become habit forming for the individual.

Remember, some addictions are the by-product of conditioning. When situations arise, something stimulates you and you respond. Over time we become desensitized, or conditioned to respond, to situations that are the same. This process leads to habituation, even addiction!

Last year I had a great discussion with Jack Canfield, co-creator of *Chicken Soup For The Soul* and author of *The Success Principles For Healthy Habits.* (Anyone possessing habituated anger should definitely read this book.) Canfield told me habits are useful in that they help people save time, but unfortunately the habits you are currently using are only good enough to get you to where you currently are!

People with habituated anger must change their habituated thinking patterns and responses. They need to challenge themselves to create new scripts for responding to situations.

Our lazy thinking patterns need to be modified!

12

Passive-Aggression

Resentment is an extremely bitter diet, and eventually poisonous. I have no desire to make my own toxins.

Neil Kinnock

Are you an individual who doesn't get mad, you just prefer to get even? Do you appear cool as a cucumber on the outside, but feel like a volcano about to erupt on the inside whenever you get into arguments or disagreements? Do you appear to co-operate with others, but inside you plot and create hidden agendas to sabotage other's plans? Do you purposely go out of your way to spread gossip and insults about others, including family and friends?

These are all signs of an individual with passive-aggressive anger.

Perhaps the best way to portray an individual possessing this type of anger is that they use it to get what they want, but they are usually unsure of exactly what they want.

Their method of operation involves taking advantage of others. Most times, people using anger in this manner get what they intended only to find out it wasn't really what they wanted. Others, who felt taken advantage of avoid them at all costs because they feel used, betrayed and humiliated.

Individuals with passive-aggressive anger behave hypocritically. They say one thing but do another. They talk out of both sides of their mouths.

Observers will catch this and over a period of time start to feel very uncomfortable around them. Those observing passive-aggressive individuals don't know what to expect other than the general outcome: I will be exploited in some way, shape or form!

From my own experiences working with this anger type, I have found most individuals possess feelings of inferiority. Some would love to take that leap toward the opposite pole of superiority, but either don't know how to or are afraid of whatever success it might bring them.

There is a famous expression that asserts, "I'd rather attempt something great and fail, than do absolutely nothing and succeed."

The second part of that expression sums up the thought process of an individual using passive-aggressive anger. They want to go somewhere, but they just don't know where. Furthermore, they are threatened by others getting to their destinations, so they don't want them to get there either!

Many factors influence the development of passive-aggressive anger, which include jealousy, rejection, experiencing abuse, feeling alienated, and failing to set positive short-term or long-term goals.

What I have learned from individuals with passive-aggressive anger is that many are mimickers or imitators.

They are less likely to step out on their own and take risks. Rather, they will try to be like others, copy others, or in some cases even try to become someone they are not!

Two exceptional Hollywood movies portray this, *Single White Female* and *The Talented Mr. Ripley*. Obviously they are sensationalized, but they offer a taste of what an individual with this anger behaves like and could possibly become.

"Passive-aggressive" is thrown around quite loosely in society, most times in accusatory joking manners. A few years ago, it became a "catchphrase". The following are examples that show passive-aggressive anger at work.

☼

Scenario #1

Charles has lived in the United States for ten years. He left Denmark after he and his wife split up. He accused her of leaving him and that she has made their two daughters hate him. He has never been back to visit, nor has he called them.

Charles took a job in a factory as a skilled tradesman upon arriving in Pittsburgh. He has worked in the same factory ever since. He has few friends and has always felt like he doesn't fit in, even though he tries.

For the last two years he has grown tired of his co-worker's jokes and Danish voice imitations. He doesn't find them funny in the least. He has never told them to stop or that it bothers him. He always smiles and goes with the flow.

This day is different. He has had enough! He joins his co-workers at the lunch table and listens to their jokes. In fact, he even encourages them to joke about him.

He glances at his watch and leaves the lunch room ten minutes before lunch is over. He goes back to his work place and gets out his blow torch. He goes to his co-workers work sites and heats their wrenches and pliers until the metal is white hot. By the time his co-workers return, the tools are no longer glowing.

Upon return, several of the workers grab their tools and start screaming. He finds this amusing. Some of the workers suffer second degree burns. Charles is accused of the offence and eventually confesses.

The company cannot terminate his employment as he has been a proficient employee. Also, he threatens to lodge harassment and racism charges at the Human Rights Commission. The company sends him to an anger-management group.

What is the cause of Charles's anger? Feeling inferior and utterly frustrated.

What are the precipitating factors? Feeling worthless and degraded. By not addressing his concerns with others, it only leads to further feelings of hopelessness and degradation, which eventually leads to his need for "getting even".

☼

Scenario #2

Jack is involved in the film industry. He has made several pitches to production companies in an effort to try and get his work produced. Each time his work has been rejected, he has been invited to submit new proposals.

Paul, a colleague of Jack's, offers him a chance to work on one of his productions. Jack is invited to the first production meeting and reluctantly accepts. He is asked to provide input in their brainstorming session.

The team is very upbeat and full of enthusiasm. However, Jack's ideas are negative and focus on the impossibilities. Paul is concerned with Jack's attitude. Several other members of the team view Jack as a "downer".

Paul meets with Jack suggesting this project is probably not a good match for him and maybe he should work on his own ideas. Jack agrees and leaves the project, he then bad-mouths the project to other friends, saying it will never go anywhere and that it is a waste of time.

What is the cause of Jack's anger? Rejection and repeated failures.

What are the precipitating factors? Frustration and rejection due to an elevated sense of self-worth. Jack is very rigid in his thinking and is not willing to co-operate with others and work as a team. Due to his inability to help others succeed in their endeavors, others will not help him with his own.

☼

Scenario #3

Stan is a 12th grader who is very popular with his male peers. He is the star of the high school football team. Stan does whatever it takes to succeed, yet he has been accused of using people to get ahead. He also has a habit of badmouthing his friends and others to make himself look better.

Recently, he asked Susan out on a date. She is an attractive, popular girl from his math class and has been at the top of the honor roll with her grades. She also belongs to many of the school's organizations. However, Susan politely declined Stan's invitation saying she was just too busy with school.

After Stan insistently pressed her for the date, she finally told him he wasn't her type. Smarting with the sting of rejection, Stan starts telling others Susan was a slut. To save face among his peers, he told them he had sex with her and that she was "too easy" for his liking. He insisted he likes good, clean girls and not white trailer trash.

The gossip quickly made its cycle through the school, tarnishing Susan's reputation. Susan's parents have sought advice from a lawyer about pressing charges against Stan.

What is the cause of Stan's anger? Rejection.

What are the precipitating factors? Stan's grandiose sense of self and his perception that he is better than everyone else. Stan also views rejection as a sign of failure and can't deal with it, so he creates situations that demean others to make him feel better.

☼

Passive-aggressive anger produces situations and outcomes of uncertainty, chaos, hurt and misunderstandings. The way most passive-aggressives deal with situations is to look at how they can twist a situation to suit themselves without any regard for the feelings of others.

Usually neither party feels good about what has happened. Those with passive-aggressive anger may feel victorious or momentarily satisfied at first, however this feeling eventually wanes and they are left with a feeling of emptiness. Especially if they have hurt or insulted someone, they are likely to feel lonely or be alone!

Having worked with individuals with passive-aggressive anger, I've noticed one particularly interesting trait that most possess: their inability to get what they really want in life.

In fact, most really don't know what they want because they tend to fly by the seat of their pants and let things happen as they may. They don't plan well. They don't think out short-term and long-term goals.

I once asked a client with passive-aggressive anger about their lack of goals. Their response caught me off guard: "It's hard to create and set well-defined goals when you have no basic working definition of yourself."

I asked this client what he meant by this and his answer was even more remarkable. "Most people like me, who are passive-aggressive are really phonies, we are wannabees!"

Wow!

Passive-aggressive anger is solely rooted in *misperception and deception.* Not only does the individual with this type of anger deceive others, but they also deceive themselves.

Perhaps the first step in the process for resolving passive-aggressive anger is for the individual to become introspective and take a deep look inward. Obviously, what is making you tick isn't working for the best. You need to know the "why" and "how" of all your behavior.

The greatest obstacle to overcoming this type of anger is to accept you are your own worst enemy. You need to realize your behaviors are based on your current thought processes that are not working. You need to modify them.

This can only be done only after you have accomplished two things:

- Knowing who you are, and
- Knowing what you really want

There are great self-help books that can help individuals find answers to these questions. I suggest taking the inner journey to find the why and the how!

13

Moralistic Anger

Holding on to anger is like grasping a hot coal with the intent of throwing it at someone else; you are the one getting burned.

Buddha

Perhaps the best way to define moralistic anger is intense "self-righteousness"! Moralistic anger is based on rigid and fundamentalist thinking.

If you possess this anger type, you probably perceive situations as:

- Right versus Wrong
- Good versus Evil
- Black and White
- Good or Bad
- All or Nothing

Almost all perceptions for individuals with this type of anger fall on a polarized continuum. Their perceptions reside at either end of the spectrum, but there is no in-between. In fact, everything is either/or with no gray areas.

For the individual with moralistic anger, they would perceive anything in the "gray area" or middle as non-committal, especially with respect to forming opinions and making decisions. They refer to those outside the constraints of their thinking process as either the opposition or fence-sitters!

The cause for moralistic anger can usually be traced back to rigid thinking, which is learned from families that are highly idealistic or extreme fundamentalists. At an early age, children learn that there is no middle ground. Compromise is out of the question! Everything is based on the all or nothing principle.

Some of the worst wars and conflicts in the history of humanity were caused by moralistic anger. Think about the Nazi Holocaust and the millions of people who were murdered in the name of a cause.

Now consider the broader discrimination and racism that is pandemic around the world. Perhaps the two greatest causes of racism are fear and ignorance. The worst part is that both are by-products of faulty thinking, which, as we know, leads to stereotypes.

These stereotypes are created because individuals are unable to think for themselves in "gray" terms. Instead, they accept force-fed beliefs that reside on polarities of black or white thinking. They are extremists in the truest sense!

An unfortunate truth is that most wars and disputes are created because of religious dogma, despite the fact that most religions, if not all, practice love and peace. When ideals are threatened, love and peace get tossed out the window and violence is seen as a means to attain peace, which already existed in the first place! Wars don't kill, people do! And these people kill because of their moralistic anger.

When I work with clients possessing this type of anger I have noticed a central tenet at root: *perfectionism*. Many are highly perfectionist in their thinking, believing there is no room for failure.

Moreover, to be wrong would indicate their failures and shortcomings. This would further reveal to them that they are indeed not perfect.

The greatest barrier holding them back from being flexible in their thinking is their fear. Individuals with moralistic anger fear being wrong. Some feel that any compromise on their behalf logically implies that their way of thinking is wrong.

Remember, these individuals think in terms of polarized positions in which there can only be two possible outcomes. They are usually hell-bent in their convictions and any shift toward the center is viewed as leaning toward the opposite pole, which they naturally oppose.

Therefore, they dogmatically hold to their set beliefs and opinions. Compromise is not an option! Any compromise equates being wrong, which translates to failure. For those with moralistic anger, convictions are set in stone and frozen in the ice age!

Read the following scenarios and see how you feel about them.

☼

Scenario #1

A local church has put together a program to bring greater awareness about the sins of having abortions. They preach that abortion is murder! Any woman having an abortion is guilty of killing her child.

They target the medical community and assert that Pro Choice centers promote and advocate abortion. They distribute information in front of these centers to women who are entering. Several times the police have been called to break up these peaceful demonstrations that have left passerby feeling uncomfortable.

A doctor in the community who performs abortions is labeled a murderer by the church group. In fact, pictures accusing him of infanticide are posted around the city. Tired of the harassment, he decides to close up his practice and move to another city.

Upon hearing this, the group is happy they have run him out of town. Still not satisfied, one of the members decides that the doctor is going to continue his "killing spree" elsewhere. Days later, the doctor is shot dead.

The member claims to have saved the lives of hundreds of unborn babies that would have been murdered by the doctor. Ironically, at his arraignment the member quotes the Commandment, "Thou Shalt Not Kill!"

What is the cause of the member's anger? An extreme sense of self-righteousness.

What are the precipitating factors? Rigid and fundamentalist thinking, which shaded his ability to discriminate between what is really right and what is really wrong.

☼

Scenario #2

A police officer races down the highway in an unmarked car. You notice he does not have his sirens on. The cop is doing well over the speed limit. What gives him the right to do this when he is not even in pursuit of anyone?

You decide that if he can break the law, then you too have the right to do the same. You start to tail him and you do so for a couple of miles. Finally, he switches on his signals and moves into the right lane, slowing down. You pass him. As you continue, he flies up behind you and pulls you over.

He asks for your license and registration. You thrust it at him and call him a hypocrite. You threaten to challenge the ticket in court claiming you will bring a complaint against the cop for speeding. When the case does go to court, you find out the cop was discretely tailing a suspect with other police officials.

What is the cause of your anger? Feeling stupid after making assumptions without having all the facts. Remember the old saying about why you shouldn't assume?

What are the precipitating factors? Possessing feelings of self-righteousness even in the face of breaking the law.

☼

Scenario #3

The government raises tuition for all university students. The costs of attending university are already high. Several students are disgruntled with the increased costs and decide to protest.

They organize a march in front of the minister's office at the government building. They picket all morning as their numbers grow into the hundreds. Finally, the police are called in to break up the unlawful gathering. They politely ask everyone to leave or they will be forced to charge violators with trespassing and disturbing the peace.

Several of the protestors become belligerent and storm the government building. Inside, they trash the statues in the foyer and spray paint the walls. They are charged. Total damage is well over $50,000. The damaged statues were paid for through taxpayers' dollars!

What is the cause of the rioters' anger? Feeling cheated and exploited by the government.

What are the precipitating factors? Believing they have the right to defend their beliefs and force others to listen. Also, since they were being "exploited", they believed they had the right to retaliate in any manner they deemed necessary; in other words, the means justifies the ends.

☼

I have found people acting on their moralistic anger to be very similar to those with passive aggressive anger. The only difference is they are more intentional and actually want recognition for what they are doing.

Like passive aggressive anger, they act first and think later. Unlike passive aggressive anger, their intentions were good but their emotions got out of control. Unfortunately, it is this latter feature that usually gets them into trouble when angry, especially when they believe they are above the law!

Moralistic anger works for some individuals when it forces them to take a stand or act when they otherwise wouldn't have. Some people are so passive others constantly take advantage of them. Others are constantly in neutral waiting for others to do their fighting or dirty work for them.

I believe most people are at their strongest and most motivated whenever their ideals are threatened. This is sometimes the kick start they need to get them going.

Some of the greatest heroes and success stories can trace their motivation to moralistic anger. These individuals, when faced with adversity, were able to rise to the challenge. They looked conflict in the eye and didn't back down.

The struggle against oppression, war, exploitation, and abuse has been a continual bestselling story for millennia. Our angry heroes do not allow their personal beliefs to be comprised and are willing to fight, even die, for them!

Remember, anger itself is not a bad emotion. It is how you use your anger that makes it good or bad. When used constructively and productively, moralistic anger has a great potential for doing good.

Some of the greatest historical movements happened because of moralistic anger, for example: the abolishment of slavery, the suffrage of women, Christianity, national independence, and even democracy.

Brave and resilient people believed in a cause and were willing to go the distance. No matter how great the challenges or the threats, these people were willing to stand strong.

In fact, they were typically the recipients of aggression but they wouldn't succumb to failure. They weren't fighting because wrong was done to them and they were seeking vengeance. Instead, they were seeking to do what was right to correct the situation.

When moralistic anger is used constructively, closed doors and boarded windows have a way of getting opened. The key to getting what you want through this anger is to know what you want and then address your intentions with others through discussions and compromise.

Moralistic anger should not be rooted in aggression and violence. It is very hard to be rational when you are irrational. Moralistic anger is one of those anger types where the rational (proper ideals) can spill into the irrational (improper behaviors).

Instead, the key to getting what you really want is to use your moralistic anger as a motivating tool to create change or correct a "wrongdoing" in an assertive, amicable, and peaceful manner, rather than provoking that wrong into greater insults.

In other words, if you are propagating peace, don't brandish a gun!

14

Manipulative Anger

Malice drinks one-half of its own poison.

Seneca

Has anyone ever referred to you as a poor sport or a crybaby? When you were a child and didn't get your way, did you pack up your toys and go home? Did you refuse to play with others who didn't want to play by your rules? Are you a sore loser? Are you any or all of the above today?

If you answer yes, then you might have manipulative anger!

What is manipulative anger? It can best be described as scheming or controlling behaviors used to get you what you want. The psychiatrist, Eric Berne, described three states people play: the balanced adult role, the parent role and the child role.

The balanced adult role is behaving and acting responsibly. You focus on the here and now. The parent and the child roles can be used in the proper context or in ways that generate dysfunction.

For example, a parent plays the parent role through nurturing or caring for their children. On the other hand, a married woman may play the parent role to her irresponsible drug using, alcohol abusing husband. She thus enables his behavior and treats him like a child!

An adult male may play the child role when he joins his friends for a game of pickup hockey. In this situation, the child role is used appropriately.

Conversely, this same man might throw a temper tantrum when he learns his wife has made plans to go out as a family the same night he had plans to play hockey. To get even, he sulks and pouts the whole night. This is playing the child role in a dysfunctional manner.

Children use anger to manipulate, so do adults!

Most individuals possessing manipulative anger usually show one or both traits of self-centeredness and impatience. Both of these traits were learned in early childhood and continue to thrive into adulthood.

The self-centeredness trait usually evolved from parents who spoiled their children and bent over backwards for them. They thought they were being great parents by giving their children everything for which they asked.

Impatience developed when the child didn't get their own way and threw tantrums until they got what they wanted. Their parents usually gave in to keep peace and shut the kid up!

I often wondered who this ploy was geared toward; trying to really make the kid happy, or giving the kid what they wanted so they wouldn't have to listen to them? I am sure most times it was the latter, which became habit.

Have you ever been out shopping and observed a child wailing and screaming as if their parents were torturing them? As you get closer to the screaming child, you hear parts of the conversation. The child is crying over their parents' refusal to buy them the cereal with the special prize inside.

Their attending parent decides to apply some quick pop-psychology they've learned from a TV expert telling them it's okay to say "no" and just let the child cry. Furthermore, they've been advised to "just ignore the child" even when they are out in public.

I've often watched this "skit" play out in the supermarket and I usually observe the same outcome. The child's face starts to turn redder as they scream louder. They eventually throw themselves on the floor and start flopping around like a salmon out of water.

People stare at the parents hoping they will do something. The parents are embarrassed, which facilitates an immediate response to make all parties happy. Into the shopping cart goes the coveted box of cereal. Case closed!

The crying stops and the child is instantly relieved. It's like a wonder drug. Fellow grocery shoppers are thankful they don't have to listen to the shrieking, sparing their eardrums further abuse! And best of all: the parent has controlled the situation once again.

Or have they? Who controls whom? If the parent was in control, then why not just put the cereal in the basket in the first place and save yourself and others the torment? On the other hand, does the child hold all the cards because they know if they scream long enough they will win?

If I was a betting man, I would back the child! This is a conditioned response the parent has created. They have taught their child, if you cry loudly and long enough I will buckle under pressure and give in to you.

The child already knows this because they have played this broken record, slow dance since they were young enough to recognize how powerful an actor they are in these situations. Basically, the child has the parent trained!

Some of the worst cases I see of manipulative anger at play is with couples coming in for marital counseling. After a few moments of counseling, you notice the roles being divided and you can differentiate the parent from the child. Interestingly, this dysfunctional "parent-child" dichotomy is usually at the root of their marital discord.

Here are a few examples where manipulative anger is at work. Perhaps you can see yourself in these situations behaving like the child?

☼

Scenario #1

You live in a dorm at college. You have a roommate. Your desk is on one side of the room and your mate's is on the other. You are listening to soft music as you do your homework. Your mate comes into the room and puts on the television set, quite loud.

Rather than ask them to lower it, you turn the volume up on your stereo. Your mate looks at you and smiles. They turn up the volume on the television. Before you know it, you are exchanging volume changes until both of you have the volume cranked up as high as they will go.

The neighbors next door are rapping loud on the walls at the ruckus. You refuse to lower the volume until your roommate turns the volume down on the television. She finally lowers it and shakes her head at you. You nod to her and lower the volume on your stereo.

You win! Your roommate gets up to leave and turns to you. "All you had to do was ask and I would have lowered it in the first place", she says.

What is the cause of your anger? Believing you should be respected and catered too in all situations, even when compromise is an option.

What are the precipitating factors? Possessing a grandiose sense of self and believing you are entitled to anything and everything you want.

☼

Scenario #2

Sam and Jane, a married couple, are having a discussion about their son. Jane makes a statement to Sam that he is never around and always working. She wishes he would make more time for their son and start attending more of his baseball games and school activities.

Sam asserts he is working hard to give both of them a better lifestyle. Jane says she appreciates it, but still wants Sam to try harder and spend more time doing things with their son. Sam becomes miffed by Jane's allegation he is not a good father.

Jane tells him she never implied he was a bad father and nor insinuated anything of the sort. Jane tries to explain her point and make him understand her intention. Sam's response is: "Whatever!"

She continues the conversation and Sam turns up the volume on the television. Insulted, Jane says she doesn't appreciate his immaturity. Sam's response is: "Whatever!" Frustrated, she tells him she's going to bed. Sam's response: "Whatever!"

What is the cause of Sam's anger? Personalizing Jane's constructive criticism as a direct attack on his fathering skills.

What are the precipitating factors? It could be that Sam realizes Jane is speaking some truth and feels guilty. Also, it could be that Sam is used to making all the decisions and feeling in control. He can't stand the fact that he is wrong and interprets Jane as being a "mother figure" to him and trying to correct him. Sam definitely has an inflamed ego!

☼

Scenario #3

Kim is a 17-year old who just passed her driver's license exam. Her father lets her use the family car, but has placed a 10 p.m. curfew for having the car home.

It is Friday night and her friends are planning to go to a dance outside of the city limits. Besides Kim, none of them has a license. They ask her if she would drive them. This is going to be the dance of the year! Anyone who is part of the "in crowd" will be there.

Kim feels the urgency to be a part of this event. By driving her friends, she will definitely be the cool young lady her friends are painting her out to be. She asks her father for the car and he has no objection other than she is to have it back by 10 p.m.

She argues it is not a school night and his demands are ridiculous. He tells her it has to be back by 10 p.m. or no car. She argues with him and makes some unruly remarks.

Offended and hurt by her remarks, he revokes the use of the car and also grounds her. Upset by the turn of events, she threatens to run away from home. Her father tells her to do what she feels she should do.

She tells him: "I'm not kidding, I will run away and you will never see me again." Hurt but appearing not fazed by her remarks, he walks away from her. She screams at him, "I hate you!"

What is the cause of Kim's anger? Getting her request rejected when she felt she is entitled to anything she wants.

What are the precipitating factors? Perhaps Kim has had it all her own way in the past and is used to stretching the limits with her father, but this time he is making no compromise. She may be used to using power plays such as threats to get her way and this time it is not working, which enrages her.

☼

Manipulative anger can perhaps best be described as a form of regression. The individual regresses into a thinking state that is based on, "Me. Me. Me!"

Early on they learned that their parent would give in if they pouted or carried on like a spoiled brat. In fact, parents unconsciously reward their behaviors, which encourages them to continue behaving this way.

There is an old saying, "If it isn't broken, don't fix it." For the individual using manipulative anger to get what they want, they don't view their behavior as "broken" or needing to be fixed.

Furthermore, even if they are aware their behavior is inappropriate but rewards them with everything you want, what is the likelihood they will be inclined to change it?

Remember, any change is going to be hard work, which will undoubtedly require a lot of thought and energy. On the other hand, if you are someone with manipulative anger, you may keep "winning" and getting what you want at the risk of pushing family, friends and people away from you.

Over time, people will become tired of your childish antics. If people keep telling you to grow up, they might really mean change your selfish behavior and be more co-operative.

Parents will say they are ready to pull their hair out because of their child's immature behavior. Just think how much more frustrating it is to deal with adults acting the same way?

I find people who behave this way often choose to remain the same and eventually wind up alone as no one can be bothered mentoring them.

Manipulative anger is often a shortcut for conflict resolution, which involves honest and mature communication. Communication takes work with the investment of ideas and feelings.

Those using manipulative anger are lazy when it comes to resolving conflicts. They take shortcuts toward a dysfunctional resolution. They only want what they want and what is best for them. They really don't care about the other person's feelings when the conflict is occurring.

In fact, these individuals tend to be conflict averse of situations that reveal their own short-comings and mistakes. Their arguing and childlike behaviors become a power play to detract from the real issues. I have found their pouting and sulking are smokescreens to try and make the other individual feel guilty and cave-in.

For those dealing with individuals using manipulative anger, refusing to cave-in means they would have to re-evaluate their problem solving skills and change them. The best course of action is to stop enabling their childish behavior and encourage them to modify their dysfunctional thinking patterns.

Some experts might refer to this as "tough love", which is often used by parents with their teenagers. Tough love is based on the ability to say one word and mean it: NO! Most parents are afraid their teens will hate them or they will push them away.

Actually, the opposite is true. Teens will learn to respect their parent's answers and learn that other people will always hold more power in certain situations. The same is true for those using manipulative anger.

Tough love is never out of vogue for any age or gender. By saying no and not giving in, you are telling others you care because you are truly doing what's best for them.

Moreover, you are telling them you no longer think of them as a child. You are an adult and you are going to treat adults like adults should be treated!

15

What Motivates Your Anger?

If you do not wish to be prone to anger, do not feed the habit, give it nothing which may tend to its increase.

Epictetus

What Motivates Your Anger?

In the lectures I teach on addictions, I cover motivation and motivational interviewing. Since people with anger-management problems posses anger in much the same way addicts possess and act out an addiction, I thought I would break it down even further into motivating factors.

There are two common things that motivate people: gain and fear. In fact, if you are motivated by extremes of gain, then you would be said to be motivated by personal greed.

Under the headings "Gain" and "Fear", take a few moments now to make a list of things by which you believe you are motivated. These could be:

- People in your life
- Things that you own or hope to own
- Activities you do
- Places at which you spend time
- Your biggest turn-ons

- Things you try most to avoid

Anything that drives you to want more, or stand to profit on, would fit under the heading of gain. Under fear, include anything you try to avoid, because it arouses anxiety or dread.

I sometimes have people asking me, "What about religion?" believing religion, moreover faith, doesn't fit under either category, that it is its own entity.

Without making a blanket statement, a Christian for example may turn to this faith because of the "gain" of salvation or the "fear" of hell. Some will argue that they believe or have faith because it is simply the factual "Truth" of life. But is truth not a gain of some sort?

Once people recognize that religious beliefs can fall under motivational reasoning, they can further introspect and determine why they have turned to religion in the first place.

Do you subscribe to your faith for reasons of fear, or are you religious because you believe you will gain something?

Remember, when someone's religious convictions are strongly motivated by fear, they are more likely to possess moralistic anger. I have found that religious fundamentalism is largely based on fear and this can lead to very irrational, egotistical beliefs, thus spurring their anger.

☼

Now return to your list of motivating factors and place them under one of three columns, as shown below:

Motivated By Gain	Motivated By Fear	Motivated By Gain/Fear
1.	1.	1.
2.	2.	2.
3.	3.	3.
4.	4.	4.
5.	5.	5.

First look at the "Motivated By Gain" column. Is there anything in your list which suggests that greed has developed?

I am a firm believer that people should strive for what they really want in their lives. There is nothing wrong with being successful and gaining more. But when does striving for success become a bad habit, even a bad addiction?

When your life falls out of balance and you are becoming a workaholic because of greed. When you are no longer functioning optimally and you have an "addiction to work" for all the wrong reasons. In essence, your passion for what you love doing gets superseded by greed.

Gain is a great motivator because it helps us achieve short-term and long-term goals. Without goals we would be living with one foot in the grave. Goals give people reasons to live and want to get out of bed every morning.

Most people who lack goals are miserable because they tend to be lost. They possess no direction. In fact, those lacking direction because of the lack of goals are people most likely to possess resistant anger and jealousy! If you possess these types of angers, could the reason be your lack of goal setting?

Gain is good. Goals are great! By focusing on both of these things in your life it leaves you little time to be miserable. Goals keep you in cruise control, preventing you from getting hung up by road blocks or recklessly racing against time!

It is when your sense of gain swells into "greed" that anger-management problems are most likely to occur. People motivated by greed are likely to find their lives spinning out of control. It is like hitting a patch of black ice at high speed and losing control of your car.

Most individuals caught in their own world of greed begin developing perfectionist personalities. The bottom line: everything becomes all or nothing. The only thing you will accept for yourself is success. You begin placing unrealistic expectations on yourself.

But this only sets you up for a world of frustration and failure. Perfectionists often use words like "must" and "should", which leaves them no room for compromise. Anything short of their stated goals means they have failed.

Unfortunately, the longer most people operate under the premise of greed the more likely they are to operate outside the box of principles and morals by which they had hoped to live.

Have you ever met someone or heard about someone who changed because they became rich or started earning a lot of money? It's as if this person changed overnight! You'd swear aliens had abducted them and robbed them of their integrity.

Money does not buy happiness for most people. Instead, they can become more miserable or miserly. Some are driven for more not because of their greed for becoming richer, but their fear of believing they do not possess enough! This is also greed.

Greed usually has at its behavioral roots aggression. Aggression is getting what you want at whatever cost. Aggression knows not empathy or sympathy. People who get in your way are steamrolled. They are viewed more as obstacles and nuisances.

Since they are viewed as obstacles, you are more likely to disregard their needs and desires. The more they frustrate you in attaining your greed-based goals, the more likely you are to act out aggressively toward them.

In fact, your perception of people as obstacles to your success could facilitate hostilities or even a hatred of others. You might grow very angry and miserable around others. Your primary response becomes one of anger.

Ever watched the movie *A Christmas Carol*? What do you think Ebenezer Scrooge was made of? He was cut from the cloth of greed!

Greed has a way of leading people to act without empathy. To be empathetic is to put yourself in another's shoes and see why they are doing what they are doing, feeling what they are feeling. In other words, empathy is trying to understand another's motivations and behaviors.

Greed does not allow for this. All empathy is superseded by the individual's lust for greater success and acquisitions. Those who are around "greedy" individuals will pick up on their selfishness and start avoiding them.

I have seen many who have the most money, houses, cars and material possessions who are the loneliest. They may never truly be alone, however deep down they are very lonely. They strive to attain more hoping this will remove their feelings of loneliness. Unfortunately, this is rarely the case.

I also have found these people with the most and who want more (the greedy types) are usually the angriest. They will tell me they dislike people because people only use them or want something from them. They have intrinsic trust issues. They can't discern between who is authentic and who is out to con them.

So rather than take a chance by trusting again, they choose to remain alone and miserable. After years of feeling alone and miserable, they want to know how they can be happy again! Furthermore, many of them recognize their "anger issues" and want to know how to overcome their hostile feelings.

I have found that most people with trust issues are this way due in part because they don't trust their own judgment. Greed has blinded and robbed them not only of their ability to be empathetic towards others, but to be empathetic towards themselves as well.

They have become so displaced from their own feelings they have eliminated the opportunity of getting in touch with their true self. They doubt their own decision making skills, which leads to frustration and disappointment. These recurring experiences lead to stress, which in turn creates misery.

Worse, over time their misery mutates into habitual anger, which the individual has a hard time shaking. Eventually, not only are they greedy and miserable, but now they have anger-management issues.

A book I highly recommend is *Cracking The Millionaire Code* by Mark Victor Hansen, co-creator of *Chicken Soup For The Soul* with Robert G. Allen. I spoke to Hansen and asked him his views on greed versus financial success. He believes greed is never solved.

His advice, therefore, is to tithe and give, as this truly gets people excited and makes them happy!

☼

Fear too is a strong motivator. Alas, fear more often than not causes individuals to act out in random and unplanned ways. Fear acted upon is usually a knee-jerk reaction.

I am sure there are situations when people need to act out of fear for survival, such as tragic situations or when lives are threatened. These are heat-of-the-moment situations which call for immediate action. Even then, looking back on these situations, most people will say they handled the matter as best they could given what they had, but wish they could have had more time to plan.

When I refer to fear as a motivator, I am asserting fear as the prime and only motivating factor for the individual in all situations. They go to work because they fear losing their job. They get married because they are afraid of being alone. They have children because they fear their biological clock is ticking.

They don't take chances or risks because they are afraid of failure. They settle for mediocrity because they might lose everything they have. They believe it is better to hold on to what they have, and not lose it, than strive for more and take a chance for something better. Throughout life they always stay in the shallowest of ends.

The contradiction about living in fear is that, for a high proportion of people, it becomes comforting and safe. They hold on tooth and toenail to what they've got! The thought of taking any kind of risk or chance is discomforting.

Conversely, those with fear as their prime motivator tend to resent the success of others who have taken risks. Here some comments they may use:

- "It's just a matter of time before his luck runs out."
- "Life's not fair!"
- "Some people get all the breaks!"
- "I was dealt a bad hand."
- "People who play the stock market or speculate are no different from gamblers."
- "We're going to pay for this later!"
- "What goes around comes around."
- "I'm safest behind my four walls."
- "Hope for the best, but expect the worst."

- "You can't fail if you don't try."
- "I'd rather keep what I have than take risks to get more."
- "If it's meant to be…"
- "No harm no foul."
- "I don't believe in taking chances."
- "I believe I am middle of the road."
- "I like things plain and simple."

Imagine living this way? What do you actually have to look forward too, growing old and dying? How depressing! A life motivated by fear creates a sense of learned helplessness. You surrender living and just exist.

Jealousy was an anger type discussed earlier, and is the most likely of all types to be motivated by fear.

People living ultraconservative lives whine and complain about others who are more successful than they are. They ask, "why them and not me?"

My answer to this type of thinking is, why not them? Perhaps they took the chances you were too afraid to take! Don't be jealous of other's success because you didn't get into the game and play ball. As Wayne Gretzky, the champion hockey player, said: "You miss 100 percent of the shots you don't take."

Fear as a motivator is usually learned from parents and families. Rather than challenging you irrational fears or lack of assertiveness, you blindly accept things as they are and how things have always been. It is sad because your goals fall well short of your ultimate potential.

In fact, some of the goals you set for yourself were predetermined by how your parents lived their own lives, ultraconservative. The latter part of the quote – "I'd rather attempt to do something great and fail, than do absolutely nothing and succeed." – becomes your unconscious mission statement.

If you'd rather be a success at nothing, is it any wonder you are unhappy and miserable? You are your own worst enemy. You resent the success and perseverance of others because you are unwilling to step out of the windowless box you live in and take chances. You get angry at yourself and then at others who are willing to take chances.

I've been asked what I would say to someone living this way. My advice is simple and honest: "Just do it and live!"

Try life! You might like it!

16

Angry Personalities

Anger dwells only in the bosom of fools.

Albert Einstein

Personality Types

Every individual has a unique and different personality. Some people are extroverted. They are emotionally expressive. They like to talk and socialize. They like to engage in a multitude of activities. They are the life of the party. They wear their hearts on their sleeves.

Others might be introverted. They keep to themselves. They don't like displaying their emotions. They keep everything inside. They avoid social situations and people. They prefer their own company over the company of others.

These two personality types are extremes.

Introverted ———————————— Extroverted

Most people usually fall somewhere in the middle between the two. If you are living in the western world, which is highly competitive and requires people to be more outgoing, being totally introverted probably won't get you what you want.

On the other hand, being excessively extroverted could also produce drawbacks. You might be accused of being too aggressive and obnoxious. This is why practicing some degree of moderation as you express your emotions is actually the optimal way to be.

☼

Introverts Vs Extroverts

How do you perceive the words "introverted" and "extroverted"? Do you have positive connotations with one or both words? Do you view one as being more negative than the other?

Since this book is about anger and anger-management, let's look at some of the nuances with each of these styles when they apply to anger.

First, there is nothing wrong with either of these personality styles. Extremes may fit some people like a glove and totally work for them. Others on the other hand may feel totally uncomfortable trying to act as an introvert or extrovert when this is not the makeup of their personalities.

Much like anger, it is how you express it or use it that determines whether it is an asset or liability!

What types of anger do you think fit with introverted personality style? Remember, introverts tend to keep things inside and have a hard time expressing or asserting themselves.

Reread the various anger types. From clients I have worked with possessing introverted personalities, I have found the following anger types:

- Resistant/Passive Anger
- Jealousy Anger
- Passive-Aggression Anger
- Manipulative Anger
- Internet/Computer Anger

All of these anger types have one thing in common: the *inability to express feelings* in a mature, honest, assertive manner. Almost everything gets locked up inside and stays inside.

What then about the extroverted personality style? What types of anger do you think fall within its domain? Here is what I have observed with my clients:

- Addictive Anger
- Compressive Anger
- Road Rage
- Conflictual Anger
- Habitiual Anger
- Moralistic Anger

Since extroverts are more emotionally ardent, their anger types would definitely reflect their persona. People who are extremely passionate about life also tend to be passionate when expressing their emotions. But some emotions expressed too passionately can be very discomforting for others. Anger is definitely one of these emotions.

Most individuals, however, do not take the time to learn, nor do they really care, about themselves and their personality styles. If it works and it isn't broken, then why fix it, right?

For those wanting to learn more about their personality styles, there are courses offered at colleges and universities that can help. Also, there are exceptional non-clinical books worth reading (See <u>Recommended Readings</u> at the back of this book).

☼

Behavioral Styles

Some psychologists and learning theorists would assert that personalities are set by the time we reach adolescence. Some believe who we are then is who we will always be. Our personalities define who we are and what we are.

I agree with these theories to an extent. I do believe we can modify or intensify our personalities through our behaviors. Behaviors are always being learned, reshaped and modified throughout our lives. They are never set in stone unless we want them to be. We can change them. We can unlearn negative behaviors we don't want or like. We are never too old to be taught new tricks!

There is an analogy I use with clients and students when discussing the difference between personality style and behavior. Imagine your DVD player is your personality. It is the hardware that plays movies. It remains the same unless you adjust the control switches on it. It can and will play only the DVD's you insert into it.

Let's say for the most part you are a movie buff like me. You watch lots of movies and are always looking for something to watch that will entertain you. After the movie ends, you remove it from the player. The DVD player remains in a state of flux until you load the next movie.

Now let's say you pick up a new release from the video store. You load the movie. Twenty minutes in you realize you've picked a dud! You're very disappointed and decide not to watch the rest of it. At this point what do you do?

Do you take the DVD back to the store? Or, do you take your DVD player to the store and complain that it plays bad movies?

The point I am trying to make is that the DVD player is like your personality and the DVDs are the behaviors your personality plays. Knowing this, a less desirable personality can now be adjusted through the modification of your behaviors. All hope is not lost!

If you want to play good movies in the DVD player, it is a good idea to read up on the movie to learn about what you are watching. If you want to act out good behaviors, then it is an even better idea to learn about the various behavioral styles you can use.

There are a multitude of behaviors people engage in on a daily basis. Most behaviors are acted out to suit the personality style of the individual, or they are held onto because some people are too lazy to change.

You always have the ability to think what you want to think and act how you want to act. With that said, you can modify or change any behavior with which you are uncomfortable.

For the purpose of this chapter, I am going to break behaviors down into 5 distinct categories:

- Assertive
- Aggressive
- Explosive
- Passive-Aggressive
- Passive

I will now discuss how these behaviors differ from one another and are unique in their own right.

☼

Assertive Behaviors

Assertiveness is the hallmark of success in personal and professional living. People who are assertive go places in life.

In fact, they get to where they want to go and further. The greatest reason for their success is their ability to behave assertively. Moreover, their assertiveness breeds the element most important to personal success: RESPECT.

People behaving assertively give and receive respect from others. They understand that in order for their own success to occur, it is beneficial to help others reach their goals. Assertive people understand empathy and how it works.

Remember, empathy is the ability to put yourself in another person's shoes and see the world through their eyes. You are able to relate to what they are thinking and feeling. If you are able to relate to their personalities, then you are more likely to understand them. If you are taking the time to understand someone, then it shows them you care and respect them. Respect is the key element to assertiveness!

To be assertive is to be goal oriented. You set both short-term and long-term goals. When you set goals, you set targeted destinations for yourself. You are in motion moving toward something desired. This is the first element of assertiveness, knowing what you want.

The second aspect of the assertiveness equation is going out and getting it. Importantly, *how* you go out and get it is the prime motivation. Assertive people get things by respecting others as well as themselves. Yes they are motivated by gain. And they rarely settle for mediocrity. They want more in life!

The equation for assertiveness would like something like this:

Being Assertive	=	Knowing What You Want	+	Respecting the Needs, Feelings and Rights of Others	+	Getting What You Want

A great book on assertiveness is *How To Win Friends And Influence People* by Dale Carnegie. The key premise of

Carnegie's book is developing exceptional communication skills based on assertiveness training.

Assertive people understand that others have feelings too. They understand the human factor. They learn not to walk over others to get what they want. They understand that lying and cheating is wrong. They reject the manipulation and exploitation of others.

Aggression and violence is not part of their problem solving make-up. They understand that open and honest communication is the best standard. Sometimes others might not like hearing what you have to say, however you gain their respect due to your honesty.

Assertive people separate the person from their actions. If someone does something wrong or bad, you bring it to their attention. You criticize the behavior and not the individual.

The assertive person separates the artist from their work, so to speak. If they recognize someone is doing something wrong, they constructively criticize to help the other person get it right.

They realize that most, if not all, situations are "win-win". If you help someone change their behavior for the better, it will also make your situation better. Assertive people realize this.

Assertive individuals do not practice shortcuts to perceptions, that is, think in stereotypes. They are fact finders and truth seekers. They use their communication skills to learn about others.

They pay attention to details and try to remain objective. They focus on educating themselves from their experiences to make themselves wiser. Truly successful, assertive people believe there are no failures. Rather, there are only lessons learned through living.

When applying these principles to their daily living, others hold them in high esteem. Others want to be around you when you are assertive. They trust your judgments. They view you as rational and objective.

Have you ever had someone come to you with a problem and they seek your advice? If you were overly critical and emotional with them, they probably grew apprehensive coming to you with future problems. No one wants to get ripped apart and criticized.

Assertive people realize this. As such, they are problem solvers. Their minds operate from a solution-focused perspective. They believe every problem possesses within it solutions and they want to find them. They know that excessive emotions blind you to the possible solutions.

Do you know anyone who flies off the handle whenever you bring your problems to them? I am guessing by now you avoid telling them your problems? On the other hand, I am sure friends and colleagues who are caring listeners enjoy both your trust and respect.

When it comes to anger, assertive people just get mad, they don't get even. They don't make impetuous decisions in the heat of the moment. They know when to take time-outs to ground their emotions. They are truly "grace under fire" people.

They acknowledge their anger and then know when to let go of it. They know how to stop their anger from running and ruining them. They recognize anger as a normal part of their lives as they do other emotions.

Assertive people know where to draw the line in all facets of their lives, including how they experience anger.

☼

Aggressive Behaviors

An aggressive behavioral style is what it sounds like, behavior rooted in aggression. Many people assume that aggression is the same as violence and that is not always true. You can behave aggressively but never become violent.
On the other hand, when you become violent you are always aggressive, that is, exceedingly aggressive!

What is an aggressive behavioral style? In many ways it looks like assertiveness until you remove the empathetic component. Empathy is non-existent in aggressive behavior. Aggressive individuals choose to become ignorant to the feelings of others.

Aggressive behavior is best described as getting what you want without recognizing or acknowledging the needs of others. Simply put, it's steamrolling over others to get what you want!

Working with clients in anger-management groups, classes and one-on-one for years has taught me that most individuals with aggressive personality styles suffer from "me first" syndrome.

Whether they actually say it or imply it, you can't miss their resounding, "Me. Me. Me!" It is almost like a tenor warming up for an aria.

People with aggressive personality styles most often seek out people with weaker personalities to dominate. Their prime candidate is someone with a passive behavioral style who will put up with their abuse!

Assertive people recognize aggressive individuals and avoid them, or minimize their involvement with them. Assertive people seek out amicable, "win-win" situations. They recognize that aggressive individuals play for keeps.

Aggressive individuals never play to lose. They play to win. You will often hear them refer to people in general as "winners" and "losers". They are polarized thinkers, where winners and losers sit at the polar ends of their continuum.

Assertive people recognize the gray areas between the poles and hope to lead those around them to the "winner's" pole. Aggressive people don't care about losers as long as they win and get what they want. In fact, many aggressive people take comfort in seeing others lose as it makes them feel more powerful.

Perhaps one of the most telling qualities of people with aggressive behavior is that *they act before thinking*. They may think a little but their thinking doesn't encompass all the potential consequences of their actions. As they are hell-bent on getting their own way, aggressive people do not consider the feelings of others.

When aggressive people are angry their emotions rule. Instead of stepping back and collecting their thoughts, they use their anger as a "super charger" to spur them even more.

Aggressive people need to step back from situations in which their emotions have disabled their ability to remain rational. In essence, they need to take a time-out.

Several anger types match up with aggressive behavior. The most common types identified are:

- Compressive Anger
- Addictive Anger
- Jealousy
- Road Rage
- Conflictual Anger
- Moralistic Anger

Bear in mind any of the anger types listed in this book could be identified as fitting into any of the behavioral styles, but there are specific types that tend to suit certain personalities.

If you ever have a chance to read any books on stress or personality types, check out Type A and Type B personalities.

Extreme Type A personalities fit with aggressive behavioral styles. Extreme Type A's are people who are highly aggressive and driven by success.

They also possess several qualities that intensifies their aggressiveness. They are more likely to be hostile. They get what they want when they want it! They are extremely competitive. Everything becomes a score card for wins and losses, and of course they prefer to be in the winner's circle.

Their motto could best be described as, "Take no prisoners!" Extreme Type A's are also very time urgent and time restricted. Everything is scheduled to the minute or the second. Lateness or unplanned delays send them over the edge.

Extreme Type A's will resort to extreme aggressive measures to succeed. When sudden-death overtime crosses them, the rule book gets thrown out and anything goes!

As for extreme Type B's, I will discuss them in more detail in the section on Passive Behaviors.

People behaving aggressively usually experience some degree of success. Many of them compromise friendships, partnerships and working relationships at the expense of their desire for success.

Do you like being ordered or bossed around? Do you like working for someone who is very successful, but likes to yell, scream and belittle employees? Do you like to feel that you need to walk on egg shells around certain people because they might get "mad" at you?

This is what it is like being around aggressive people. Most people are too afraid to confront the aggressive individual because they are afraid they might get chastised or even physically hurt.

Furthermore, those that do confront the aggressive individual usually find their constructive criticisms met with resistance, disbelief and accusations of jealousy, insecurity or stupidity!

Remember, the true essence of the aggressive individual is to get what they want without empathy for others. Aggressive types become their own worst enemy since they push away those who really care. People eventually grow sick and tired of being belittled. People grow weary of being taken for granted.

Highly successful aggressive types usually have clones around them who want to be like them but have no loyalty. When the harsh reality of isolation sets in, as it always does, they ask themselves, "Why doesn't anyone like me or care about me?"

Because they have pushed everyone away!

☼

Explosive Behaviors

Explosive behavior is very similar to aggressive behavior except with an added couple of sticks of dynamite, gasoline and matches added to the mix! People who are over-anxious and quick to fly off the handle possess explosive behaviors.

Doctor colleagues of mine assert that explosive behavioral types are those who run a higher risk of cardiac events, such as heart attacks and sudden death, and tend to have elevated blood pressure (non-essential hypertension) with no clear biological cause. Could it be that their angry thoughts boil their blood?

Like aggressive behavior types, explosive personalities are Type A. They get what they want, when they want it, how they want it, at whatever the cost. They do not care who gets in their way. If people get hurt, they view them as "casualties of war".

People with explosive behavioral styles show no sign of guilt, remorse or shame in doing what they do. They possess few, if any close friends. If they have associates and colleagues, they only associate with them because they have something to gain from them.

Most people are too afraid to be near them. They have probably witnessed episodes of aggression or violence and worry they'll be next. Moreover, some people are just too embarrassed to be around them because of their spur of the moment tirades.

Some of the anger styles that are often seen in explosive behavioral types are as follows:

- Compressed Anger
- Petrified Anger
- Addictive Anger
- Habituated Anger
- Road Rage

- Conflictual Anger

Of all the behavioral styles discussed, explosive personalities need to learn behavioral management strategies that teach assertiveness training. For all the explosive behavioral types of clients with whom I have worked, the first thing I have taught them is how and when to use "time-outs".

Just as a parent has to monitor their child's behavior when they are misbehaving, these individuals need to parent themselves. They need to learn how and when to step back. They need to learn to teach themselves when enough is enough.

Unfortunately, most individuals who behave this way are very reluctant to seek help and make changes. From my own experiences, as well as other professionals with whom I work, they only seek help when they are mandated to by the courts or when they believe this is their last chance to save their marriages or jobs.

Usually they are looking for a quick, makeshift solution to fix their problems. They come in for counseling to change others. They receive counseling to make the courts and attorneys happy. They seek counseling to learn ways to sweet talk spouses, family members, bosses, and co-workers. Rarely do they ever seek change because they believe they need it.

People with explosive behavioral styles are a lot like alcoholics: They need to lose everything and hit rock bottom before they will seek help.

However, I truly believe that if they are sincere about changing, anything is possible!

☼

Passive-Aggressive Behaviors

I've often been asked what the ultimate motive or goal is for the passive-aggressive individual? This is tough to answer, I would assert passive-aggressive people get what they think they want, but are rarely sure of what they really want.

Their desires are very much like the autumn weather. They change from moment to moment, thoughts and ideas blowing in the wind and in constantly shifting directions. Because they are never sure of what they really want, those around them are at a total loss too.

Passive-aggressive individuals resemble people with aggressive behavioral styles in the way in which they pursue what they want. They too walk over others to satisfy their needs and desires.

Furthermore, they are more likely to use and manipulate others. In the beginning, others might not be aware they are being used, but when they do catch on they disappear very quickly. Passive-aggressive people have few, if any, close friends. No one trusts them!

Have you ever been used by someone? Were you able to ever trust that person or respect them the same way you originally did?

People are smart and eventually get tired of being played. In the end, passive-aggressive individuals usually find each other. Ironically, they become critical and leery of each other, which may be poetic justice!

Some of the anger types associated with passive-aggressive behaviors are:

- Passive-Aggression
- Moralistic Anger
- Manipulative Anger
- Conflictual Anger

Aggressive people are quite straightforward when it comes to expressing emotions. They say what they intend to say whereas passive individuals say little or nothing. You rarely ever know where you stand with them. Rarely, do you ever feel comfortable around them. They probably feel uncomfortable living in their own skin.

I have counseled many individuals possessing passive-aggression. Those who actually admitted having a problem had introspected long, hard and deep. What most reported was a deep seated hatred of making decisions and taking positions.

Some said they were forced to make major or serious decisions early in life, which led them to grow uncomfortable when taking sides. Some said their inability to make decisions spilled over into other facets of their lives, which made them fence-sitters.

Many individuals with personality disorders have at the core of their disorder passive-aggression. It could be that one manufactures the other as much as it compliments it. Ironically, it is their narcissism and perfectionism that ultimately prevents them from seeking help.

The key element for change for passive-aggressive people is to enhance their decision making skills. Once they master their ability to make decisions for themselves, soundly and rationally, their manipulative, standoffish manners are greatly reduced. They no longer carry the hidden agendas they are accustomed too.

Furthermore, the need to use and manipulate others evaporates. They learn how to say what they mean. Their goals are defined and everyone involved with them is aware of what they are seeking. They are able to attract and keep people interested in them.

They are no longer perceived as threats!

☼

Passive Behaviors

Passive behavior is very similar to passive anger. Passive behavioral styles can best be summed up as never getting what you want unless you like wallowing in misery.

Passive individuals tend to always get used because they allow others to rob them of their rights. They get mad at others for using them and mad at themselves for allowing themselves to be used.

Passive individuals never seem to get what they want. Unlike passive-aggressive people who are uncertain about what they really want, passive people know what they want but are afraid to go out and get it. In fact, they allow others, likely aggressive individuals to use them and control them.

Passive individuals whine about how unfair life is. They allege to be victims. Unfortunately, they like to play the victim role because it gives them something about which to complain.

Some of the common anger types associated with passive behavior are:

- Resistant/Passive Anger
- Internet/Computer Rage
- Jealousy
- Petrified Anger

The most common element associated with passive individuals is their sense of *learned helplessness*. They truly believe they are in situations beyond their control.

Moreover, they believe they are forced to stay there. Some like to play the martyr's role whereby they allow others to enable their passivity.

Recall that aggressive individuals are most likely to possess extreme Type A personalities. The opposite is true for passive individuals. They are most likely to possess extreme Type B personalities.

Type B personalities are likely to possess attributes opposite those of Type A. Most Type B personalities are very carefree. They get exploited and used by others. Some recognize it, while others are totally oblivious to it.

Extreme Type B's rarely budget their time well. They may wait to the last minute or run out of time because of poor time management. They get frustrated because they procrastinate and then, when things are due, they get flustered by other's expectations.

Some Type B's let others usurp their time, resulting in no time for themselves. But they are likely to complain that no one respects their time!

Type B's are non-competitive and are more likely to miss out on things they want. They may even refer to themselves as losers and laugh about it. Sadly, deep down inside many really do feel like losers.

Much like aggressive behavioral styles, passive individuals require courses, workshops and books on assertiveness training and esteem building. Most passive individuals discuss change, but rarely ever follow through. Like aggressive individuals, they usually have to experience some major life event, tragedy or adversity that will motivate them toward change.

Many passive individuals are afraid of change. They dread the potential failure that may ensue through re-creating themselves. Many have known repeated failure and can't imagine the thought of experiencing new kinds.

Working with passive clients has taught me that some people actually find solace and comfort in misery. This feeling becomes a kin they would rather hold on to than something new and unknown. An individual suffering from chronic depression with whom I once worked offered something very profound:

"The only feeling I have ever known is depression. How would I ever recognize what joy is? And if I did and it was as good as people say, would it not make me more depressed if the joy was suddenly taken away from me? For this very reason, I would rather remain depressed!"

As this outlook makes sense to the individual with depression, I am sure it also fits with passive individuals. Passive individuals feel extremely helpless or believe others control them.

Yet even though most are aware of how they perceive the world, they do little to change their "hopeless, helpless and hapless". They are content to play the role of victim because it gives them a sense of mastery and control (albeit a masochistic one) over their lives.

I have spoken with medical doctors, psychologists, psychiatrists, and nurses who have pointed out that those with extreme passive behavioral styles are more likely to complain of being sick, tired, run down, possess nagging aches and pains, and depression.

Passive individuals are most likely to be characterized as sponges or receptive canisters for other people's demands. They take in other people's garbage, which builds and builds until it overflows. These individuals feel like they are drowning in a toxic vat. These toxins poison them with thoughts of helplessness and depression. Some become so overwhelmed it incapacitates them.

Have you ever been around someone who projects a lot of negativity and despair? Do you enjoy listening to someone constantly complain about their circumstances? How does it make you feel?

Most people feel completely drained being around passive people. I refer to people such as these as "psychological or psyche vampires" because they leave you emotionally sapped.

Most assertive people have a very low tolerance for passive people as they do aggressive people. People get tired of carrying conversations, perhaps even relationships. Explosive types have next to zero tolerance for passives, as do passive-aggressive people.

Interestingly, aggressive behavioral types thrive on passive people. They complete each other's utter dysfunction!

When you look at relationships where domestic violence exists, you can usually find one of the partners being the aggressive type while the other one is the passive type. In fact, you might view the aggressive individual and passive individual as one in the same but on different ends of the continuum.

       Aggressive   ————————   Passive
  (abuser/enforcer)   (victim/receiver)

Many victims of abuse learned to be passive from abusive and dysfunctional parents. They were taught to rely on others for nearly all facets of their lives and become dependent. Hence the term "co-dependency" arose from this type of dysfunctional relationship.

In my book *Why Women Want What They Can't Have* I explored the dynamics and factors of relationships and abuse. I strongly recommend reading it if you have repeated failed relationships or are currently in a dysfunctional one.

Passive individuals need to take assertiveness training workshops. The source of their problem is low self-esteem, which leads to feelings of inferiority. When you build your self-esteem you become more self-sufficient and self-directed. This will get you out of the doldrums of passivity and into the world of assertiveness.

Remember this flowchart:

I Think It --- I Feel It --- I Act It --- I Become It!

Translated into positive and accountable terms:

I Think Assertive Thoughts --- I Feel Assertively --- I Act Assertively --- I Become Assertive!

Try it. What do you have to lose?

17

How To Manage Your Anger

When angry count four; when very angry, swear.

Mark Twain

Manage Your Anger

Everyone gets angry at some point. Anger is not a bad emotion, it's how you act and use it that makes it detrimental.

With that said, most people do a pretty good job at managing their emotions. On the other hand, there are those who don't and require new strategies for keeping their anger in check.

Over the past fifteen years, the most rewarding experience I have had counseling clients with anger-management problems is when they stop coming for counseling because their anger is in check. The anger-management strategies I am about to discuss are based on the techniques I use in counseling.

I often create anger-management plans with clients, offering them a variety of strategies. Most of the time, the client and I decide on a plan that is best suited to their personality and behavioral style.

Over the years, I have modified and use 8 anger-management techniques:

1. The Big Adios
2. Laminated Reminders
3. Perspective Taking
4. Own Your Feelings!
5. Stay in the Present
6. Parroting
7. Cathartic Sublimation
8. Deflecting

I hope one or more work for you if you are having difficulty managing your anger.

☼

The Big Adios

I have been asked many times whether or not walking away from a situation when angry is just running away from your problems?

My response is a resounding NO!

Remember, you could do more harm than good if you choose to remain in your current situation. If you are the explosive or aggressive type, if your anger lands you in trouble with the law, your boss or with your family, then "exit stage left" is probably the best option for you. It is better to have a job or family tomorrow and think things through rationally, than throw it all away in a New York minute!

Psychologist Dr. Albert Ellis has written an excellent book on the subject of anger-management, *How To Keep People From Pushing Your Buttons*, explaining how you can change your thinking patterns and modify your aggressive behavior.

It is important to remember, though, the strategy of walking away shouldn't be considered a "fix-all" and used in all situations all of the time.

This strategy is a bandage solution until you get anger-management counseling and support. Eventually, you will have to get to the root of what is making you angry. You can't run from everyone.

Remember, conflict is good, in that it brings to the forefront the need for change. If you run whenever conflict or adversity stares you in the face, you will miss out on opportunities for personal growth and positive change.

Removing yourself is the best option when you run the risk of becoming violent or hurting someone. The people from whom you are escaping will probably be those who see you angry most of the time or push your buttons. Should they ask you where you are going, the best advice is to say nothing or that you'll talk with them later when you are calmer. Let them know you are upset and then beat it!

At this point, if you both haggle over who is going to get in the last word in, you run the risk of recreating the situation as it usually begins and ends, out of control!

Keep in mind that you are the one with the anger-management problem. It is not your concern at that moment how the other person feels. It is more important to recognize how you feel and get out of there before letting your anger loose on them!

Laminated Reminders

This strategy was suggested by a client who was charged with assaulting his girlfriend. He had a very prominent position in society, both with his career and the volunteer organizations to which he belonged.

One drunken night he slapped his girlfriend in public during a minor argument. He was charged with assault. It was the most embarrassing experience he had ever encountered. The incident even made page three of the local newspaper.

At the court hearing, the judge instructed him to get anger-management counseling. This is when he came to see me. We discussed what happened and how he was feeling after the incident. Fortunately, his girlfriend had forgiven him. All of the organizations he was involved with were also forgiving. He wanted to know what interventions he could put in place so an incident like this wouldn't happen again.

After a couple of sessions, I learned from him that after he has a couple of drinks he becomes aggressive. I also learned that his greatest motivator was the fear of losing everything he had worked for. That is: he was driven by greed.

He was greatly humbled by what happened. This incident was a blessing, in a sense, because it knocked him off his pedestal of greed. He was now motivated to change, shifting to the realization that gain, not greed, was a more acceptable motivating factor.

Together, we came up with a game plan. First, he would have no more than one drink when out in public or with his girlfriend. I suggested he avoid drinking all together, as his drinking was a by-product of needing to unwind from his professional life.

We also discussed the "greed factors" he possessed. He agreed that if he took his foot off the accelerator and went to cruise control then he wouldn't have to drink to take the edge off.

In subsequent sessions we also discussed the reasons for his intense desire for success. We discovered the self-esteem issues that were causing him to feel inferior. Months later, when these revelations were unraveled and accepted, greed became non-existent.

The second part of the plan was something we devised based on the technique of "aversion therapy". In the initial duration, he needed something that would serve as a daily reminder for what had happened. He acknowledged that the write-up in the local newspaper made him sick to the stomach. It gave me an idea – "News Clipping Aversion Therapy"!

I had him make several miniature versions of the article and laminate them like credit cards. He was to carry one in his wallet, glove box, brief case, and anywhere else he would regularly see it. Also, if he went to the bar, he would take it out and place it next to his wallet as a reminder.

This approach worked! It produced the results he wanted. He later mentioned there were two occasions where the card dampened his aggression before it ignited. Six years later, he has managed his anger without becoming aggressive or violent.

For those who want to try this approach, I encourage you to write down on one side of paper your fears (in regards to anger), and on the other side something that makes you feel good (a loved one/child), or something spiritually motivating, and have it laminated as a card.

Remember, for this to work it has to be something that touches your heart and mind. It has to motivate you.

Give it a try; what do you have to lose? Don't be tomorrow's local news story!

☼

Perspective Taking

In this approach, I teach clients what it feels like to be in another person's shoes. This approach is very much like assertiveness training.

In assertiveness training, a key element is reflective listening. Reflective listening skills are at the heart of perspective taking and can often de-escalate conflict and confrontations before they get out of hand. Most reflective listening training and skills come from the work of Carl Rogers and his Client-centered Therapy approach.

The two major ingredients for reflective listening are:

1. Listening with intention/active listening
2. Paraphrasing

1. Listening with Intention

Listening with intention requires listeners to become active participants in the conversation, not only in speaking but also in listening. When most people communicate, they think of what they are going to say or how they will answer while the other person is talking. Rather than fully devoting their undivided attention to the speaker, they are contemplating possible responses.

Listening with intention involves just what it implies. You listen to both the denotation and connotation of the speech.

Denotation is the surface level dialogue others offer us when they speak. Denotation is the simple spoken word. The gist of what is said.

Connotation, on the other hand, is the emotional, subjective meaning underlying the words. Connotation provides the ingredients that gives words true meaning. Always remember, words don't mean, people do!

To listen with intention means listening for the true meaning within spoken words. Rather than analyzing the words themselves, active listening requires the listener to seek out the true intention for what was said.

This approach works in anger-management because when you focus on the intention of words spoken, your mind no longer has time to dwell on confrontational and aggressive responses. If you are always waiting for the chance to respond to further fuel an argument, intentional listening might save headache and regret.

Sometimes people say things they don't mean or say things in the heat of the moment without thinking first. Their subjectivity over-rides their objectivity. Many prolonged arguments and fall-outs are the result of misspoken or unintended words. If you are the type of individual who possesses conflictual anger, then situations such as these are prime catalysts for your ire!

Remember, you are the one with the anger-management problem and it is not the other person's fault for getting you all bent out of shape and "making" you aggressive. You are in control of your mind and body. How you decide to respond is up to you.

No one can make you angry!

That decision is totally up to you. If you have a personality that thrives on conflict and manipulation, then you are probably eager to counter-attack during arguments. In fact, you are most likely to strike low or launch stored up grievances at the other person.

Listening with intention helps to redirect you from your conflictual, aggressive thought process. When you are too busy listening with intention, you are distracting yourself from your own irrational thought process and your need to argue.

Here's an example. What if I told you, "It's raining cats and dogs."? If you listen without intention, then you are just listening to the spoken words. You might react with, "Big deal!"

However, when you listen with intention, you might hear something more than just the spoken words. I might have uttered this statement because I care about you: it's cold and rainy, and I don't want you to catch a cold.

Argumentative people, though, usually focus on the superficial meaning and prepare to say something sarcastic in return. "Do you think I'm blind? I can see it's raining!" They may even feel the other person is being insulting, that they are incapable of taking care of themselves.

Notice how easy it is to disagree over something we are in total agreement with?

2. Paraphrasing

Paraphrasing is another tool of reflective listening. Paraphrasing is the process of seeking clarification or reaffirming what the other person has said. It is putting into your own words what the other person has said. It clarifies the true intention and meaning of what has been said.

This alone can minimize misunderstandings and prevent ugly arguments. More so, clarification is important because it guards against the word ASSUME. That is:

ASS / U / ME

Reaffirming also emphasizes the process of reflective listening. It allows the listener to stick to or alter their point of reference. If you agree with what the speaker has said, then you can attest to what they are saying.

Should you disagree, then you can protest what is being said. Either way, it lets the speaker know you are listening instead of firing preformed responses.

If you go back to my original example, "It's raining "cats and dogs", paraphrasing would clarify and reaffirm the spoken meaning and the intention of this statement. For example:

Statement: It's raining cats and dogs.
Paraphrase: It sounds to me like it's really raining hard.
Clarification: If I hear you correctly, you are concerned for my wellbeing and you don't want me to get wet.

The individual with whom you are having this discussion can now respond with either agreement or disagreement.

The major goal of perspective taking is to keep the lines of communication open. If you possess aggression, practicing this approach shows others you are open-minded and willing to listen.

If you were to continue to practice rigid thinking and be less responsive to others, you will soon get the label "stubborn" or "hardhead". People will not want to talk to you because they know all you want is to argue.

Perspective taking gets you out of your combative attitude as it encourages listening and obstructs argumentativeness. If you want to improve the quality of your relationships and social interactions, I strongly recommend this approach.

☼

Own Your Feelings!

Whenever I counsel clients, one of the first points I emphasize is that nobody can make you angry unless you allow it.

Not surprisingly, clients object to my "ridiculous" statement. I usually smile and ask them if they think I could make them do something against their will. I've even gone so far as to ask, "Could I be your God and make you do whatever I want, even make you angry?"

Of course they think about it for a moment. But before they are ready to answer, I badger them with another question: "Do you think your wife, husband, boss, or whomever makes you mad is God over your life?"

They usually offer me a very definitive "No!" I then have them stop and rethink what they were trying to convince me of a moment before. Here is the line of reasoning I show them:

"Okay, it is your spouse or boss who makes you angry. So, if they can make you angry, then they are responsible for all of your other emotions as well – joy, sadness, fear, etc.

"Just think about what you are telling me! You've convinced yourself that others are responsible for your emotions. This means you must be an empty shell waiting to be fed and filled by others.

"Worse, once filled you relinquish control. They can now make you dance around however they choose, not too unlike a monkey dancing around the organ grinder. They truly are God to you. How does that make you feel?"

At this point, there is often a prolonged moment of silence, usually broken by a nervous laugh, snorting, head-shaking, or knee slapping. The response I hear next is almost word-for-word identical for each client, "Wow, I never thought of it that way!"

Once more, there is usually a prolonged silence and, almost like clockwork, the next comment they make is virtually the same: "It's only my wife who gets under my skin." "It's only my husband who annoys the hell out of me!" "My kids are on my last nerve." "I hate my boss and my place of work!"

Remember the list of the people, situations or things that make you angry at the beginning of this book? I am sure it's the same person or situation that most frequently heads your list. It might seem they were put on this planet to purposely annoy you, but it's not true.

Rather, you have created an "anger script" with this person whereby you make them the villain or source of your angst. You give them power they don't possess. Even if they did have some power over you, it is how you choose to *respond* that determines their degree of mastery over you.

I want you now to remember the following:

- You own your feelings and only you can feel your emotions.
- No one can control you unless you let them.
- Even when you let someone control you, you are still in total control as you choose how you will allow them to manipulate you.
- Accusing others of making you mad or creating other emotions is an attempt to escape responsibility for what you are thinking and feeling.
- No one, including yourself, can make you feel angry unless you first think something to stimulate your emotions.
- Only you can decide whether to get angry or not, just as you can decide to get sexually aroused or not.
- The mind can only devote its full attention to one thing at a time! If someone around you is trying to engage you in a conflict and you are too busy fantasizing about some tropical oasis, the likelihood of you getting upset isn't very high!
- Those with whom you get angriest are usually people close to you in which you have a vested emotional, interest.
- Perhaps the reason you are really getting mad is you wish to be the puppeteer (controller) and others are not co-operating with you!
- Why should everything always have to go your way or be the way you like it? Perhaps you are a

perfectionist putting too much pressure on yourself and others!

In perspective taking I discussed active listening while engaged in conversation. It turns out that when you own your feelings, you actively listen to your thought process!

What are you telling yourself to make yourself angry? There must be something. Others can't annoy you unless you perceive them as an annoyance and you make yourself upset at the thought of them. Perhaps you have a stereotypical mental script for each person with whom you relate in your daily life?

Situations always turn out the same because your thoughts, actions and behaviors are scripted on previous encounters. Moreover, if you are using repetitive scripts with the same individuals, they are probably doing the same with you.

In a sense, we are very much like Pavlov's dogs. Over a period of time we behave in the same way in response to the same individuals. This is because we perceive them as remaining in a flux state (stimulus) and we fail to apply an active thought process to how we react to them (response).

When you and your spouse argue or fight all the time it probably looks like the same movie playing itself over and over again. Do you see the same cast of characters? Do you see the same scene or plot?

I want you to reflect on the example of the organ grinder and the monkey. Who actually controls who? Does the monkey dance because the organ grinder plays the music? Are people amused by the monkey jumping around? Or does the monkey dance to make the organ grinder play more music? Who looks sillier?

In repetitive domestic disputes, there is always an organ grinder and a monkey. Which one are you?

If you choose to own your emotions, no one can control you. In fact, you start to gain better control over your own thought process. You no longer become a sideshow, rather a very polished performer!

The choice to think, feel, act and become is always yours.

☼

Stay in the Present

Most people get a great sense of comfort from reliving emotions and experiences from the past.
Interestingly, the emotions and experiences are not always pleasant ones! Some people prefer to hold onto negative experiences because it gives them a sense of perceived power or comfort. As discussed earlier, this is at the root of petrified anger!

Why do so many people choose to live in the past? The answer is quite simple: The past is comforting because it is non-threatening. They already know what has happened.

In contrast, the future can be daunting because we have no control over it.

Ironically, the same holds true about the past. We have no control over the past because it has already happened. We cannot go back and change it!

The only timeframe over which we possess control is the present. What I find interesting when I work with clients is their resistance to feeling and existing in the present. The reason is they have to invest time, energy, thought, and emotion to change existing negative thought patterns. For some, this is quite threatening, not to mention hard work.

They hold onto what they know even though it is detrimental and negative, rather than risk gaining something more positive. Generally speaking, when it comes to self-analysis and change, most people choose the lazy chair.

If you are an individual possessing a habitual and petrified anger-management problem, you need to get out of the past. Time traveling machines exist only in the movies. You can't go back and change things in real life. Your anger-management problem is here and now and requires change!

Keeping your emotions in the present state is paramount when you are involved with people who have wronged you in the past. Reliving the affronting situation in your mind only gets the juices flowing, the pulse racing and the angry thoughts recurring all over again. You need to stop this if you are ever going to move on!

There are several questions to think about when discussing anger:

1. How can getting angry today undo what happened in the past?
2. How can getting angry now making you feel good in the present?
3. Can you actually go back and change what happened?
4. Do you think those who did wrong to you still dwell on what happened and get as upset as you do?
5. Do you believe you are in control of yourself right here, right now, in the present?
6. If you answered yes to the last question, what do you want to feel right now? What would make you feel great?
7. If vengeance or harm is wished upon the person from the past, then you are not living in the present! How can you get into a positive, present feeling state now? What is a positive, happy thought for you now?
8. What goals would you like to set for yourself that will make you a "present" thinker?

Hopefully you can begin to recognize a few things:

1. You can only control the present.
2. Only you control your thoughts, feelings and actions.
3. The past will always remain the same, unchanged.
4. Your present will soon become the past and wouldn't you rather build on healthier pasts?
5. Anything you choose to be or do is up to you.

This exercise teaches autonomy, empowerment and hope, especially when used daily, hourly, and moment-to-moment.

Once you do this enough times, living in the present becomes second nature. Importantly, living in the present distracts your thought processes from drifting back into the past.

You can't think of past wrongs done to you when you are thinking about feeling good right now!

☼

Parroting

Parroting is an interesting approach that works well for individuals with compressive anger, in particular those who are screamers.

I learned this approach by watching children get their way with their parents. It is a tenacious, "wear them out" approach that gets results!

When you were a child did you ever drive your parents insane during long car rides asking repeatedly, "Are we there yet?" Do you remember how crazy this use to make your parents? They were willing to do just about anything to shut you up! Being a nag actually does have its virtues on occasion.

What is important to remember is that you possess the anger-management problem and you will try using this approach to prevent yourself from blowing up and screaming at those who push your buttons.

Parroting works just as it suggests. You repeat the same thing over and over again until you get what you want. You are not hurting, harming or threatening anyone. In fact, you are basically asserting your intention on the other person and leaving it up to them to respond.

This approach works remarkably well if you are a parent having difficulty getting your kids to listen to you. I have taught this approach to several clients. They have used it with their children, tweaking it here and there. In the end, it usually produces favorable results. Kids start doing what they are asked to do so their parents will stop nagging them!

A great success story for this technique involved a client I had a few years ago. He was married to a woman with a teenage son from a previous marriage. The son did not like him and would often start arguments between his stepfather and his mother.

My client had an anger-management problem that was deeply embedded in compressive anger. He claimed he could go from zero to sixty in under a second. He would erupt at his stepson whenever he didn't do what he was told. The teenager would never do his chores due to laziness and defiance. This would set my client off when he came home from work.

Things would escalate into a war between him and his wife. One night he actually grabbed the teen and shook him around. His wife threatened to leave him if this ever happened again. My client came to me looking for ways to control his anger when his stepson defied him.

I explained the parroting method to him and he agreed to try it, even though he wasn't convinced. He was instructed to remain calm next time a chore was not completed. He was to approach the son and sit next to him and politely point out what he didn't do. If the son still didn't complete the chore, he was to follow him around all day and night, nicely bringing it to his attention. He even stuck little post-it reminders around the house!

Apparently his wife was not impressed with the approach, but if it prevented him from getting angry with her son then she agreed to co-operate. He even took it one step further. He called the school to speak with the principal. The principal called the boy to the office and said, "The lawn needs to be cut!"

His son was so embarrassed, and fearful that it would happen again, that the first thing he did when he got home was cut the lawn. I should also add that my client's wife is now using the same approach with my client.

What goes around comes around!

☼

Cathartic Sublimation

Catharsis means to release or relieve stress. Sublimation means to direct your aggression toward socially acceptable activities.

Sublimation is a psychological defense mechanism used to direct unacceptable sexual feelings or aggression onto something that society views as acceptable. For example, instead of punching your spouse or kicking the cat, you go and strike a punching bag.

Cathartic sublimation is great for those with lots of stress and frustration. In fact, this approach is highly recommended to all, even those without anger-management problems. It's a great method for stress reduction.

Here is a list of some of the activities my clients swear by:

- Working out/exercise/sport
- Walking/hiking
- Meditating
- Martial arts
- Comedy (television/movies)
- Swimming
- Gardening
- Listening to music
- Shopping ("Retail Therapy")
- Weekend getaways/vacations
- Long drives
- Reading
- Painting
- Playing with pets
- Praying
- Napping

Since everyone is different, it is best to select a cathartic activity you find most relaxing and non-taxing. Just taking a 15- to 20-minute walk each day will do wonders for calming your mind and body. Also, if you are cooped up in doors all day, I recommend getting outside and enjoying the fresh air.

The key aspect of this exercise is to remove yourself as far away as possible from the rigors of everyday living. You might call this a brief vacation from reality.

Give it a try, it may work wonders for you!

☼

Deflecting

Deflecting is one of the more interesting techniques developed for people with severe anger problems. It also works very well for those who have a hard time taking criticism, even when it's meant constructively.

Deflecting is not a technique for the squeamish. It requires the individual with the anger-management problem to remain cool, calm and composed for it to work. It's is great for recreating the dynamics in relationships with those whom you have detrimental conflict and anger issues, but it requires patience, practice and persistence.

Earlier I discussed how many relationships possessing conflict and dysfunction operate like a movie replaying itself time and again. Those involved are like actors playing the same roles over and over. Solidified cognitive scripts are played out without thought. The argument begins the same way, plays out the same way and ends the same way.

Perhaps the greatest instigator of personal insult and anger is name calling. If someone makes fun of your appearance, weight, flaws, defects, you take it to heart. It hurts.

It hurts even more when it comes from someone close to you. When you get into heated discussions with family and friends, it seems they have a way of yanking hardest onto your heart strings. They know your vulnerabilities and use your past transgressions to sting you, even though they claim to have forgiven you. It's as if they have stored up grievances to be used as ammunition against you during arguments!

If you are the individual who erupts when someone starts attacking you, then deflecting may be your best line of defense. In fact, it may be the best and only anger-management technique you may ever need to use.

Remember, this approach is used by individuals with anger-management problems when dealing with others who know how to provoke them. It is a great approach for modifying "lazy" argumentative scripts. More so, if you change your script then the other person will have to change their own because it no longer produces the same results or ignites the same response.

This is how it works:

First, you will need to re-train your own thinking process.

Do this by telling yourself that individuals who verbally attack you are insecure and desperate. This is the honest truth. If someone has to try and put you down to make themselves feel superior, it's because they have low self-esteem, plain and simple. Once you give in to put downs, you increase their perceived superiority over you, so don't fall into this trap.

Try to view the individual attacking you as emotionally delayed in their social skills. Perceive them as a little child requiring attention. If a child calls you names, you are less likely to take it to heart, are you not? Do the same with adults who try to put you down. Once you see them as a child in an adult's body, thank them for whatever they are telling you, or pleasantly agree with them.

The following is an example from a client with whom I worked whose wife was emotionally abusive toward him. After being goaded into arguments, he would literally come out swinging. He was growing more physically abusive each time. The couple really did love each other, neither wanted a divorce, a real case of "can't live with them, can't live without them!"

Here was what he claimed his wife was doing to send him over the edge:

"My wife calls me names all the time. She is a fitness fanatic, and I am not. As you can see I am very much overweight. She calls me a fat pig! She tells me I'm disgusting. She says I am a terrible lover. She makes fun of my manhood! She makes negative comments about my family. I recently got laid off and she says I am totally useless. She says I'm a loser. Funny part is, I really do love her and she says she loves me! I really do feel bad whenever I shove her or hit her."

How would deflecting work in this situation? How could it help change this detrimental and abusive condition?

Even though he kept claiming every argument was his wife's fault, I informed him that he had the ultimate control over his emotions and actions. By controlling himself and choosing to change his responses, he would inadvertently motivate her to change. In fact, both would realize she could no longer "control" the situation as he put it.

I offered him this deflecting technique. Although at first he was wary of trying it, deflecting taught him the following ways to respond without aggression:

1. Perceive your wife as a big kid who feels insecure, especially when she makes derogatory comments.

2. You are to take each insult and turn them around into constructive criticisms. You will thank her for pointing out your shortcomings. For example, when she calls you a fat pig, your response will be: "Thank you honey for pointing out I have a weight problem. I am glad you are concerned for my well-being."

3. You are to act and appear sincere when responding to insults. Avoid showing displeasure or anger. When someone senses this, they smell blood in the water! When the next round of attacks happen, offer a short smile with a kind, agreeable statement such as: "Gee honey, you've really pointed out some things I need to work on. I love you for that."

4. If and when you feel your anger boiling, remain calm and walk away offering a gratuitous statement such as: "Sweetheart, you've given me lots to think about and I will go and do some thinking right now. Thank you."

5. Parting shots will almost surely be fired your way. Whenever this happens, say nothing or tell the person you, "I love you too."

Always remember, you are the one with the aggression or compressive anger problem. You can't afford to lose it and hit the other person!

As you use this technique and become more comfortable with it, use mild humor and smile whenever someone rips into you. It shows the other person, at least outwardly, you are not bothered by put downs.

Remember how your teachers used to tell the students to ignore the class clown? By ignoring them, the clown would realize that no one was stimulated by their antics and they would be forced to move onto something more stimulating, hopefully schoolwork.

The same is true in relationship disputes. The other person will realize your triggers can no longer be manipulated and they will have to find more mature means of capturing and holding your attention!

The client in the above example used this technique to change the dynamics of his marriage and saved it! His wife was forced to modify her own behaviors. They now have two children and everything is much better. This is not to say they don't argue anymore. It is *how* they argue now making the difference!

Remember, the key attributes required when using this approach are patience, practice and persistence. There is no going back once you start. Otherwise it reaffirms the other person's belief that they can provoke you at will!

You have to work through it, but over time I believe you will get the positive results you want.

Happy deflecting!

18

Children and Anger

Anybody can become angry - that is easy; but to be angry with the right person, and to the right degree, and at the right time, and for the right purpose, and in the right way — that is not within everybody's power and is not easy.

Aristotle

One of the growing complaints I hear from parents and teachers today is how angry children are becoming! I am constantly informed of the plethora of workshops and organizations focusing on childhood bullying. Why is there so much aggression and bullying going on in children and teens?

Colleagues and parents with whom I have spoken have a number of hypotheses.

Some believe it is due to the high incidence of Attention Deficit Hyperactivity Disorders (ADHD), along with other pediatric mental-health disorders.

Others assert it is due to the media. Kids are watching more television shows and movies that promote sex and aggression. The most popular types of video and Internet games for kids are usually laden with violence.

I have also heard parents argue the rise in childhood aggression is because of incompetent teachers and poor educational systems. On the other hand, I have heard several teachers assert it is due to insufficient parenting skills and discipline.

I believe it is a combination of factors. I would cite some of the reasons just mentioned, but having worked with families, couples and children in therapy, I do believe the ultimate cause of angry children is rooted in dysfunctional families.

From what I have experienced, three distinct precipitating factors stand out:

1. Communication within the family circle is non-existent or minimal.
2. One or both parents, as well as older siblings and extended family members, use aggression regularly and this is witnessed by younger children.
3. Children are being verbally, emotionally, physically, or sexually abused.

Anger follows a simple law of nature: You can't get something from nothing! Anger in children had to be born from something.

Let's examine each of the three factors I mentioned.

Lack of Communication

According to some experts, did you know the average amount of time that parents engage in effective and productive communication with their children is under 10-minutes per day?

Every time I hear statistics like this I am floored! Is it any wonder children lack self-discipline skills? Furthermore, is it any wonder some children feel neglected enough to use anger as a means of getting attention?

The best parents are those who recognize they are both part of the problem and part of the solution when they have kids with anger-management problems.

If you engage your children in active communication on a daily basis, you will know what your kids are thinking and feeling. Help to shape their lives instead of shipping them off to someone else. Love and appreciate your children instead of neglecting their emotional needs.

Neglect fuels anger because children get tired of feeling abandoned and unwanted.

☼

Witnessing Aggression in the Home

How can anyone witnessing aggression and dysfunction behavior on a regular basis not be affected by it? Children who grow up in homes where anger is a staple emotion expect it. They start to view it as the norm for thinking, feeling, behaving, and acting.

Children observe aggressive behavior from those they model or adore; that is, their parents. Over a period of time they learn that aggression works for getting what you want. Monkey see, monkey do!

If you act like an ape, your child is most likely to become like you. Remember, you taught them to swing from the tree! For as long as I have been a therapist, I have never counseled a client from an extreme dysfunctional family who didn't possess some kind of depression, anxiety or personality disorder.

Parents can help facilitate positive personality growth in their children if they recognize their own dysfunction. As you work through your own anger and aggression problems you are administering preventative medicine for your own children so they will not become the next generation of aggressors.

If and when you are told by others to get family counseling, anger-management or some kind of social support to remedy family dynamics, I strongly advise you take this input as constructive, helpful criticism.

Moreover, when you see your child acting out and getting into trouble, this is a sign that an intervention is needed. Things need to change before they worsen and get out of control.

Preventative medicine is the best approach!

☼

Being a Victim

I have mentioned that I've never worked with a client who witnessed dysfunction on a regular basis and went on to develop a healthy psyche. Most victims of abuse grow tired of it and eventually snap.

I have heard from experts that children abused at home usually take it out on other children or teachers at school. Conversely, children who are bullied at school are more likely to abuse younger, smaller siblings, even their parents.

Being abused and constantly witnessing violence creates cold, hostile aggressive feelings. Remember the old expression: You are what you eat! When you are fed something long enough, you eventually become it. You get fed enough vile and violence, than that is what you will become.

Parents perpetuate violence in their own children by constantly abusing them. Abuse is wrong! Remember, your kids look up to you. You are their primary role model. You need to set the example for them to live by.

I chatted with Dr. Bernie Seigel, the doctor best known for his work with children and patients suffering from terminal illness. He truly believes in the healing of the soul and the promotion of love. He especially promotes this concept in parent-child relationships. He believes parents should always persist in loving their children and emphasizes loving behavior.

If you are loving your kids, you are not teaching them anger and hatred!

KIDS AND VIOLENCE

I appear regularly on major news talk radio shows across the United States and Canada. Recently, I did a series of guest appearances following yet another shooting massacre in San Bernardino on December 2, 2015 ,leaving 14 people dead and another 22 injured. I was asked about how parents and teachers should even go about discussing incidents such as these with children, as well extreme acts of anger.

Having worked with children's organizations, teachers, and other educational institutions, I find that adults need to be honest with children, but also not too cliché. Adults should avoid sounding philosophical, but rather do their best to reassure safety themes.

I also stress telling children that what happened was a very rare occurrence, and that there are not bad people, rather people who choose to do bad things. I try my best to educate adults and kids not to use stereotypes or labels. The same should be done in cases like this.

When discussing events that make the news or have traumatic repercussions in society, it is always best to start out asking children what they have heard, or what they know about what happened. Get it in their words, as well as what they believe/think happened. Avoid discussing details that are very graphic or allowing children to see images, as this can become very traumatizing for them. Furthermore, do not let them spend time following news stories on television or the internet.

Younger children have a tendency to personalize what happened. They are more likely to ask, "Can this same thing happen to me?", or "Are we in danger?", whereas teens are more likely to make things political, based on stereotypes (i.e., exhibiting racism, politics, sexism, religiosity, etc.) Reassure them what happened, happened far away and that they are safe. Furthermore, inform them that police and law enforcement officials are hard at work doing their jobs to protect people, and prevent things like that from happening again.

Although children maybe young, they are not stupid! They hear things and it is important that they get proper information and reassurances.

There are many great books focusing on children and behavioral/anger-management problems. Please see the <u>Recommended Readings</u> appendix at the back of this book for more information.

19

Tired of Fighting?

The world needs anger. The world often continues to allow evil because it isn't angry enough.

Bede Jarrett

Anger is a normal healthy emotion. It is how you use it that makes it productive and helpful, or destructive and detrimental.

To be angry is to celebrate your humanity. You have the right to think, feel and act. No one should ever tell you not to get angry. That is your right. In fact, more people should get angry. Perhaps this would initiate the changes that are needed in today's society!

Anger is a sign that something is discomforting and change is needed. Most people are afraid of change and avoid it like the plague. Interestingly, most would rather get angry and bitch about the way things are, than get angry and try to make a difference.

Anger signifies dissatisfaction and a call for action. Use your anger assertively, productively and with good intention. When you use your anger with positive intention, you will strive toward win-win situations!

Today, bullying seems to be at an all-time high: rampant in schools, workplaces, social settings, in homes, and on the Internet—on-line social media such as Facebook, Twitter, Instagram, My Space, e-mails, texting, etc. With all the public service announcements, education, and knowledge with regards to bullying, why are so many people still being victimized? Conversely, why is it that so many individuals of all ages are turning to bullying and abusing others?

BULLYING AND ANGER

The famous psychotherapist Alfred Adler was very fond of using the concept and phrase "INFERIORITY COMPLEX' to denote how one believes they do not measure up to the standards which others, society or they themselves have set. Many people who have inferiority complexes experience this as children, when they were bullied, shamed, or rejected by parents and/or significant others. For some, they internalize these feelings and beliefs about being inferior, thus carrying it into their adults lives. Many will become shy individuals, even passive. Unfortunately, too many will develop mental health issues such as anxiety, depression, learned helplessness, and even *Personality Disorders* (See Diagnostic and Statistical Manual of Mental Disorders, also known as the DSM-5). Luckily, a large portion will overcome their inferiority complexes, outgrow their shyness, become more extroverted, and live very successful lives filled with self-confidence and great self-esteem.

Adler also came up with the antithesis of the inferiority complex when he coined the concept "SUPERIORITY COMPLEX". For some, they developed the superiority complex as a defense mechanism to overcome or counteract their inferiority complexes. If you study psychoanalysis—the school of psychology that Adler came from and the one Sigmund Freud was the "Father" of—you will learn they love using concepts surrounding defense mechanisms to explain or understand why people often times behaved irrationally or offside!

For individuals possessing a superiority complex, they have a grossly over-exaggerated perception of themselves. Referring back to the DSM-5 under personality disorders, many will develop *Narcissistic Personality* type disorders, and in extreme cases, *Borderline Personality Disorder*. Furthermore, in kids and teens, often times when this starts to evolve into a problem, they may possess *Conduct Disorder* (more common in males) and/or *Oppositional Defiant Disorder* (more common in females). None of these disorders are good or beneficial!

Often the trajectory for those with a superiority complex has as its end destination or bulls' eye, BULLYING, as they become the bully. The only way that makes sense to them is to use some form of aggression to achieve what they want. This aggression can be physical, verbal, mental/emotional, and even spiritual in nature.

Bullying usually occurs in at least one of two ways. It can be either direct (face to face with the individual) or indirect (when the person isn't there). Indirect bullying would include gossip, slander, back-biting and purposeful exclusion from a group's involvement, which often happens in the workplace or at social functions. Today's generation of bullies are becoming more proficient in indirect bullying as so many are using the internet via Facebook, Twitter or text messages to attack victims. Online social media has become a major avenue for some to carry out their bullying as it provides a sense of safety, anonymity, and sense of control. You might say that those who use social media to bully are more likely to have passive-aggressive personality styles.

Physical bullying is the most visible and appears to be the most common type people see and discuss. These are physical attacks on the victim which include incidences from poking to punching to strangling and even stabbing someone. Obviously, when one engages in physical bullying there has to be direct contact, and the victim is present to receive the physical abuse. This style of bullying and abuse is used by individuals who rely on physical intimidation and/or domination, and who possess anger management problems.

Bullying can also be psychological/emotional in nature. Much like verbal bullying, psychological bullying cuts deep as well, perhaps deeper! This type of bullying involves the systematic diminishment of another individual. When you do this to another person, it can leave profound, yet damaging scars. When someone engages in this type of bullying, it can range from mild to severe, as well as sublime to extremely obvious. Often times, these behaviors would include ignoring people on purpose, isolating them from the group, rejecting them outright, thus not making them feel like they belong, or terrorizing other people at work or in social settings. For those being bullied in this way, they often times feel very helpless, misunderstood, hated, and even ugly.

If you or someone that you know is the victim of bullying, the worst thing that you can do is nothing. Many times it has been asserted that adults "just need to work it out", or "ignore it and it will go away". If you are the one being bullied or sexually harassed at work, and the bully continues to engage in harassing you, and you have tried working it out, do you think it is easy living with what is going on? Often when incidents of extreme bullying continue, co-workers and supervisors need to get involved.

WHAT CAN YOU DO TO STOP BULLYING?

What can co-workers, supervisors, and friends do when someone is being bullied? Interventions need to occur immediately before things become ongoing and habitual. It is important to get all of the facts and then act for the benefit of the one being abused or victimized. You can help victims of bullying by doing the following:

1) Listen carefully to the victim if they are willing to talk. Often they need to be heard and you might be the one they have chosen to speak with.

2) Talk to the victim about their options in dealing with the bully. They have three options: they can try to ignore the bully; be forthright and up front with the bully; or report them to the supervisor at work. If it is a case of abuse in the house, unfortunately reporting the situation to the police/and or leaving for a safer haven many be the last or only option.

3) In cases where adults lack self-confidence and suffer through issues of being more assertive, they could take college level/general interest courses in self-esteem building, assertiveness training, and communication skills building. There are also wonderful support groups that cover these

skills in communities and on-line. Interestingly, self-defense courses are designed to improve confidence and mental strength as well and this is also a valuable option!

4) It is important to ask victims what other kinds of help they think they might need. They might need to speak to a counsellor, therapist or psychologist, especially if they possess anxiety or depression.

5) It is important to watch for changes in one's behaviors and actions that conflict with one's normal personality. If there is a marked change in one's moods or attitudes, there is most likely the need for open communication and you shouldn't pry, but rather inquire as to why someone appears to "not be themselves".

TYPES OF ABUSIVE OR DOMINATING BEHAVIOR

Since writing the original *What's Your Anger Type?*, I have been contacted by thousands of people sharing their experiences with anger either as the one with the problem, or the one experiencing another person's anger. Many of these personality/behavior types I am about to outline are seen in many, if not all, bullying situations.

Here is a list of seven, very similar to the anger and personality types that I discussed in the book, but worth mentioning within their own right. I refer to them as power plays, as I am an avid hockey fan, and power plays give one team the man-advantage. In this case, power plays are used to gain advantages over another through unfair manipulation, bullying, neglect, or abuse.

1) *The Gunnysacker* - Gunnysacking is all about one keeping a silent journal or mental notes about the wrongs someone has done to them; perceived wrongs done against them; things others have done to irritate them; or stored up hurts, angers, grievances and past conflicts to be used at a later date. When that later date comes, they erupt and everything that was bottled up explodes, even in what appears to be over a non-threatening discussion or incident.

If and when you are on the receiving end of the explosion/tirade, you are very confused and perhaps even frightened by how someone can literally snap over what appeared to be nothing. This is not about the actual event that the individual erupts over, rather a by-product of their "COMPRESSIVE ANGER'. You see, they never discuss or vent what they are angry about. They may be very passive in nature by all accounts. Then when they can't hold down the bottled up stress or frustration which lead to anger, they blow their cork, and usually pick on safe targets. Once they realize they can get away with doing this to certain people—someone they perceive will take it—they are more likely to make this into a habit. They use or pick on certain people to vent their anger out on. If this is a personal relationship, a partner is often surprised as they thought everything was fine in the relationship, that is until the person blows up.

2) *The Belt-Liner* - This personality type is in some ways much like the gunnysacker in that they enjoy storing grievances up and using them to punish someone at a later date. They may have had issues with you or someone in the past, may have even vented their frustrations or disproval, but they cannot seem to let it go. They have difficulty in forgiving and forgetting, even though they may tell you that

all is forgiven. When they are having a bad day or feel in the mood to argue or create conflict, they dig into their bag of mixed emotions and throw in your face something that you did to wrong them in the past.

This "power play" is used to degrade, shame or embarrass the other person. They often times will use this belt-lining tactic when they have an audience to really make the individual who is their target that much more humiliated. Individuals who behave and bully others using this power play often are very aggressive to passive-aggressive individuals. They are always just one insult away from letting it all out. They get a sense of mastery, satisfaction, and power from berating others as this builds them up.

3) *The Moralistic Castigator* - This personality uses their rigid, fundamentalist thinking—usually very religious or politically-based—to chastise and belittle other people. They believe they have the right to judge or shame people publicly based on their religious convictions. Their internalized goal is to humiliate others in front of others, while believing they are doing a service to this person by correcting them.

The individuals are often fanatical in their beliefs and their moods change from one moment to the next. They listen with intention for ways to verbally attack others and draw them into arguments or conflicts with the sole purpose of winning the debate. They suffer from inferiority complexes, and their moralistic castigation feeds their inflamed egos thus allowing them to feel a sense of superiority.

This personality type is very aggressive in nature and a verbal bully. They often times feel the need to drown people out in conversations by speaking over them, or getting louder to intimidate. They are very insecure people, usually not well-read or informed, or only choose information that is one-sided and best reflects their current trending thought patterns. As a result of this, they are not rational, rather emotional and having conversations with them is a waste of time as you often feel verbally abused or insulted.

4) *The Sulker* - This personality type is pretty evident in that the individual takes a very unique approach to conflicts, debate, confrontations, etc., in that rather than discuss matters rationally, they choose to sulk. They are very passive-aggressive individuals who actually control the situation by coming off as portraying themselves as passive and vulnerable.

They are able to manipulate and control situations by sulking or pouting, and this helps them get what they want. Their goal is to make the other person feel bad, even a bully! The other individual often says "I am so sorry I made you cry or become upset; I feel so bad now..." This plays right into the sulker's hands as they know what they set out to do—manipulate others or the situation in a passive-aggressive manner—has worked. This is all a game to the sulker in that they do not want to investigate integrity or honor in discussions, negotiations, or resolutions. Rather they prefer to play the role of victim and get outcomes handed to them on a silver platter.

5) *The Stormer* - The Stormer is one who "storms" out of conversations, discussions, or disagreements when they do not get their own way. It is all about making a scene and being a "drama king" or "drama queen". With these

individuals, it is all about power and domination in that they feel the need to control others as well as the conversation. They are much like The Sulker, but they are aggressive rather than passive-aggressive, playing the role of the passive.

The Stormer definitely possesses a superiority complex. They feel the need to be correct in all discussions, get people's approval, and have control at all times. When they do not feel as if these needs are being met, they put people down as "idiots", "stupid people", and belittle others, making them out to be insignificant. They derive a sense of satisfaction from doing this in front of others, or an audience whom they believe will side with them.

6) *The Rager* -This personality type is one that is mad at the world. They find flaws in everyone and everything, and they are always looking for arguments—to start them, find one, or finish one. Much like the angers, as discussed in this book, their personality type, when it comes to displaying anger, is often based on shame and rejection.

They possess a superiority complex which is rooted in feelings of inferiority. I like to refer to them as possessing "Little Big Man Syndrome"—this applies to both men and women—in that they are like a little Chihuahua and they project themselves to come off barking and biting (i.e., bullying) like a Rottweiler. A good friend of mine who is an exceptional canine trainer in Canada once told me that little dogs have no idea how big they actually are, and will be willing to take on big dogs. Interestingly, Ragers often know where they stand in relation to others, but are not willing to accept their shortcomings or work on themselves in constructive ways to create more amicable behaviors based on their thoughts and feelings. Instead, they prefer to rage to mask their own shortcomings.

7) *Framers* - Framers are passive-aggressive types; if you recall, I discussed them earlier in the book. They are all about themselves in that they try to make themselves look better at the expense of others. If that behavior is not required, then they try to play the innocence or victim's card and make things all about themselves.

They are all about getting attention and sympathy. Normal, assertive people appreciate empathy. Framers want you to feel sorry for them or their situation. They are passive by nature, but often times tend to shift toward being more passive-aggressive when they are not getting the results that they are seeking.

I have given you anger management strategies for dealing with your own anger or the anger that other people demonstrate. The various strategies will also work for these power plays, and next time you find yourself in a distressing situation with someone who is using them, I suggest putting them into play immediately!

Bullying is a serious issue and it affects all ages: kids, teens, young adults, adults, and seniors. There are excellent resources and free books on bullying that you can download now at www.bullyingisforthebirds.com.

The purpose of this book is to help readers with anger-management problems realize they can control their anger and it need not control them. The key points to take with you can be summarized:

> You always own your emotions.
>
> No one can make you mad.
>
> Anger, like any emotion, will not last forever.
>
> You need to identify triggers for your anger.
>
> Life is too short to stay mad.
>
> Just as there are differences in people, there are differences in anger types.
>
> Find the anger-management technique that works best for you.
>
> Seeking arguments will most likely initiate anger.
>
> Never go to bed angry.
>
> You can feel whatever you choose to feel.

☼

Anger Inventory

Now that you've finished reading this book, you can apply the principles and strategies to your own life. I suggest reading this book through again, especially the chapters pertaining to you.

Over the next 30 days, keep a log of events, situations or instances when you feel angry. Fill out the form below. I recommend duplicating this form so you have several copies for each day in which you do these exercises.

ANGER INVENTORY

1.	What types of anger do I possess?
2.	With which situations/people precipitated my anger?
3.	On a scale of 1-10, how did I handle my anger today?
4.	(Very important!) What was I telling myself or thinking about at the time I got angry? What was my self-talk which made me mad? Take 5-10 minutes to relive this situation and meditate on it.
5.	What could I have done differently instead of getting angry?
6.	What can I do next time a similar situation arises? What thoughts do I need to retrain?
7.	What anger-management strategies work best for me?
8.	Which one should I learn/practice?
9.	Is there an anger-management support group I can join in my community should my anger problems get

worse?

10. Is there an "anger-management buddy" I can find to whom I can vent whenever extreme situations arise? Perhaps a therapist?

Parting thoughts…

You can choose to be angry or you can choose not to be angry! If you get angry, how will you express it?

SECTION TWO

TECHNOLOGICAL RAGE

MILLENNIAL ANGER

TECHNOLOGICAL RAGE
Millennial Anger

ARE YOU ADDICTED TO TECHNOLOGY?

TEXTING TORMENT

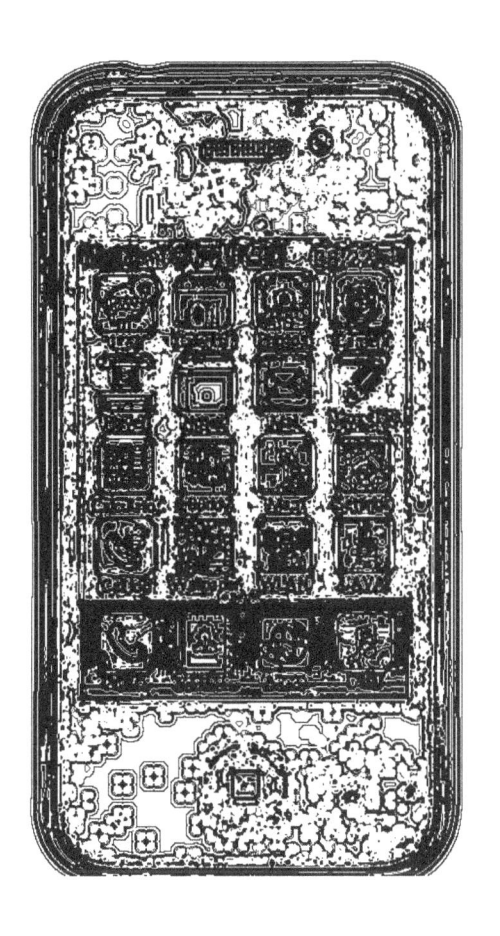

Do you have texting rage? In the last couple of years the amount of text messaging has exploded off the chart in terms of how many people are participating. The research I have undertaken has demonstrated a tremendous rise in the amount of females addicted to texting. Furthermore, the rates of rage tied to women who text is on the rise. I refer to this phenomenon as "texting rage"! To find out whether or not you possess aspects of this type of rage or a lot of this rage, please take a few moments to engage in the following questionnaire:

1) I find that one of the first things that I do when I wake up in the morning is I either have to check my phone for a text message or I need to send one.

5 - Always
3 - Almost Always
1 - Sometimes
0 - Never

2) I find that I cannot go more than 15 minutes without checking my phone to see if I have a new text message.

5 - Always
3 - Almost Always
1 - Sometimes
0 - Never

3) I find that when I am driving, I cannot resist the need to text and drive at the same time, even though I say I am not going to do it.

5 - Always
3 - Almost Always
1 - Sometimes
0 - Never

4) While driving, I sometimes take chances texting even though it may result in a ticket or being non-courteous to other drivers.

5 - Always
3 - Almost Always
1 - Sometimes
0 - Never

5) I text in places that could get me into trouble or where I disrespect other people such as at work, school, or social events.

5 - Always
3 - Almost Always
1 - Sometimes
0 - Never

6) I text other people who are in the same house or building as myself rather than just walking to see them in person to say what I need to say.

5 - Always
3 - Almost Always
1 - Sometimes
0 - Never

7) I get angry/agitated whenever I text someone and they take longer than I expect or want them to take to return my message.

5 - Always
3 - Almost Always
1 - Sometimes
0 - Never

8) I get angry/offended whenever I text someone and they text me back, hardly taking the time to answer my text appropriately, or use the same amount of time I put into my text.

5 - Always
3 - Almost Always
1 - Sometimes
0 - Never

9) Texting with others has created disputes, misunderstandings, or fights with others.

5 - Always
3 - Almost Always
1 - Sometimes
0 - Never

10) I believe there are or should be certain rules and standards to texting and everyone should follow them.

5 - Always
3 - Almost Always
1 - Sometimes
0 - Never

The highest total you could score is 50! If you scored 50, there is no doubt that you have an anger or rage tied to text messaging. After speaking with a large number of people who text and who have experienced anger as a result of their texting, I arrived at these common scores or standards which may assert one has an anger problem tied to texting:

40-50 TEXT MESSAGING RAGE
29-39 ADVANCED TEXT MESSAGING RAGE
19-28 GETS FRUSTRATED EASILY WHEN TEXTING
9-18 SOME FRUSTRATION WHEN TEXTING
0-8 COULD CARE LESS ABOUT TEXTING

If you scored 29 or above, you may want to consider for yourself whether you have some issues surrounding communication that is inclusive to technology. It is interesting to point out that even though many people possess this texting sort of rage, they do not have it in their everyday conversational interactions when it comes to face to face communication, or even speaking on their phone, including cell phones, for that matter. I found that very interesting!

In my book *What's Your Anger Type?*, I was the first many years ago to coin the term "Internet/Computer Rage". In my opinion, this texting rage is nothing more than a continuation of rage based in another form of technology. Here is a little refresher on some of the key aspects of "Internet/Computer Rage":

☐ You're waiting for the URL site to change and you're growing impatient

☐ Your screen freezes and you start pounding the mouse or keys

☐ Pop ups keep appearing on your screen and you start swearing

☐ Your e-mail is overloaded with junk mail and you start cursing

☐ Blind ads are sent to you and you actually reply with nasty e-mails

☐ You participate in internet chat to precipitate arguments, otherwise known as "trolling" ☐ You have to constantly surf the 'net to get your fix or else you go into withdrawal and get very irritable

☐ You start stalking others in chat rooms or through their e-mail

☐ You've actually punched your monitor when things were moving too slowly or have frozen

☐ You've actually picked up the monitor and thrown it at the wall or out the window

These were actual symptoms and acts of Internet/Computer Rage that people reported experiencing when I interviewed them or saw them in private practice. I recall one individual in anger management counseling—they will definitely remain nameless—who was so irate when their screen froze that they picked up their monitor and threw it out a window of an office building. They forgot they were on one of the higher floors and nearly hit a pedestrian below!

Getting back to texting rage, many of the causes of the symptoms are similar, but they are usually based on impatience and misperceptions. Before I discuss this in greater depth, first you have to understand just as the "rules" surrounding internet communication were blurred or not formally defined when it first came out, the same lack of rules applies for text messaging. Let's face it, there are no text messaging courses formally offered in university settings that provide a learning experience along with credits for how to text properly. Could you imagine? Gee, many adolescents—not to mention young adults—would score as geniuses in these courses! Interestingly, in my experience as a professor/lecturer, I've seen that some students cannot stop them self from texting, even for an hour in my courses. I know because I watch them!

Furthermore, some people—usually in this same age bracket—cannot refrain from texting while driving. This I have seen firsthand as well as heard from my police friends. This bad habit—which I might add is illegal—is adding to road rage, another anger type I discussed in my book *What's Your Anger Type?*

In terms of impatience and lack of understanding for what proper protocol is for text messaging, the implications lead to episodic anger or even addictive anger when it comes to some people and their texting. This becomes their psychological battlefield. Some people take the whole process too personal!

Back in the day, which was less than 20 years ago, you either had to talk in person or on the phone. Also, written communications were of the postal service type, affectionately known now as "snail mail". What these methods all had in common was a commitment to getting one's point across—getting their message out in the context it was intended. Text messaging, as well as e-mails which first were "guilty" of this phenomenon—though not to the extent as text messaging—are being sent, whereby intended messages are incomplete, misconstrued, or badly typed/spelled by the sender of the message. People are texting out of habit, mostly on autopilot. In fact, most are trying to get as many words on the tiny face of their cell phones in as short of a period as possible. What does this mean? Words are being communicated in shortcuts, abbreviations, icons (e.g. lol, ;=), etc) and this is confusing to many. Do you know why? Texting is creating stereotypes, also known as shortcuts to perceptions. When this happens, people begin assuming. And when people assume, they are doing so from their own vantage point of perception or how they are currently feeling/wanting to interpret something. Also, text messages contain little if any emotion because they are just too short. What does this mean? Once again, the receiver of the text is often left to decipher or interpret the feeling behind the text...ah, not a good thing! What kinds of problems do you think this is causing?

Do you also remember back in the day when several books and theories were written about differences that exist in communication between men and women? Women were viewed as the more effective/emotional communicators who sought answers at a deeper level, while men operated at the surface level. All bets are off with this as texting has narrowed the differences with today's generation as both genders spend too much of their communication time texting; there's not enough face to face communication and this is creating poor social communication skills all around. While doing my research, I might add that women/females tend to text more than men! Women who once loved the underlying meaning within communication and spoke the same emotional lingo are emotionlessly degraded to texting. And at the time of writing this, doing research and receiving personal information on texting, it is not uncommon for females and probably some males to send as many as 20,000 to 30,000 texts per month! Yes, you read correctly: two different friends reported text histories with daughters running up those monthly text tallies. And the ramifications are? Communication skills—no matter if you are male or female—going down the drain!

When someone sends out a long text message, after investing so much time and thought, and gets back a short or one word answer, this drives some totally irate. "I am only worth a one word answer?" they ask themselves. Also, some become incensed when they diligently respond to texts sent to them but others take "too long" to respond. In this instance, they feel they are not a priority and this makes them feel neglected. I hope you are beginning to see a pattern forming with texting and anger.

I would also like to add that texting has led to another can of worms: texting/cell phone crimes. The FBI refers to these evolving mobile phone crimes as smishing and vishing. According to the FBI, smishing is a crime created through combining phishing (the act of trying to attain usernames, passwords/pass codes and credit card information) and SMS texting (short message service texting), also known as text messaging: today's hottest addictive behaviour! Added to this is also the perps' abilities to use voicing and phishing as well (calling your cell phone and asking you for this information directly).

How do texting crimes (smishing and vishing) work? Criminals contact you through phone messages, text messages or e-mails. They "inform" you that there is a problem with your current account information involving your technological device and if it does not get corrected immediately, you will lose your service as well as all of your information surrounding that service. The worry about service loss induces some people to give the information criminals are asking for instantly: credit card information/numbers, PIN information, bank account numbers, mailing address, landline phone numbers and some even ask for Social Security information.

The information you have provided to these perps gives them access to your bank accounts, credit cards, and personal histories. Within minutes, money is often drawn out of your bank accounts or purchases are made using your credit card. If the perps plan on doing this ongoing, they might only skim continual small amounts from bank accounts which make the theft undetectable for a long period of time. Many instead will go for the big hit and rob you of as much as they can at one time. If that doesn't scare you, in some cases the perps go so far as to steal your identity!

Texting is here to stay, at least until some more modern form of communication occurs, perhaps some kind of technological telepathy; at least if this could be mastered, the art of communication would improve infinitely as everyone would be able to read your mind. Wait! That could be a very bad idea as well. So, in the meantime, if you want to continue texting, perhaps you can make the experience a little more enjoyable, rather than addictive, as well as better understood instead of confusing. After interviewing hundreds of people who text, and listening to both their successes and frustrations, I have come up with these potential solutions which might make the process more effective for you.

> *"I can't wait to get to the next red light so I can check my cell phone! Red lights have never been this fun before, other than in Amsterdam!"*

POSITVE ETIQUETTE FOR TEXTING
RULE #1
Always text in complete sentences whenever possible! Take the time to convey the true message you are sending instead of sending it in piecemeal or "smiley" faces (even though they're cute) the receiver may not understand what you are truly trying to say.

RULE #2
If and when you have a very important message, take the extra few minutes and make a phone call! Even if the other person is not available to talk, you can leave a full detailed message in their voicemail and they can receive the full intended message.

RULE #3
Whenever texting and you know this will become your last message, go "military" which basically means, leave it with something like "over and out!". This is a courtesy that lets the other person know you are done texting and they will not wait around for further replies and getting frustrated when nothing more comes.

RULE #4
Don't begin a conversation, especially one of importance, and then disappear or say TTYL which is texting for "Talk To You Later". This is surely one way to annoy someone!

RULE #5
Don't text and drive! Besides the obvious that it is illegal and distracting, many misunderstood messages get fired off that way because you are in a rush to get a minute message out in a fraction of the time.

RULE #6
Never text someone who is in the same room or the same house as you. There is no better word than "pathetic" to describe this behaviour. It is all about respecting a person enough to make face to face contact with them. So many people told me that this made them feel degraded because they felt they were only worth a text.

RULE #7
Put the damn phone away! Too many people literally eat, sleep, walk, talk—with other people...that is truly displayed in restaurants—and need to text. This behaviour borders on "addiction" or could already be an addiction. You know you have issues with your texting behaviour when you can't even go to the bathroom, bathtub, shower, or have to check your phone at every stoplight. Stop the insanity!

These are simple and very basic rules for texting which you would think, if not assume that most people would understand. Unfortunately, many people do not get it! I am hoping that by reading this they will get a better grasp for extending common courtesies when it comes to texting.

ONLINE SOCIAL NETWORKING

Over the last two years I have been inundated with radio and TV requests to appear on shows to discuss a plethora of topics surrounding online social networking venues such as Facebook, Twitter, My Space, Internet chat rooms, etc. Often my appearance on these shows is not to discuss the "warm and fuzzies" of these site experiences, rather instead some of the acts of aggression, even violence, resulting in deaths of people. (Just Google "teen suicides related to teen bullying".). One of the more sobering shows I appeared on occurred last year when a larger radio station hosted an afternoon-long forum on teen bullying, suicides related to bullying on-line, and what could be done to prevent it, or stop it from happening again. One mother's story about the death of her daughter really brought to light that something needs to be done!

What is it about online social networking sites that ramps up aggression and even violence? From what I have learned, researched, and heard from hundreds of people are that two things facilitate this occurrence: Anonymity and Instant Gratification.

Anonymity is perhaps the hallmark of aggression, personal assaults, and conflict on-line because the internet never puts you face to face with the other person unless, of course, you are using webcams. You can say and do things and not be accountable for the ramifications of what you do. At least these people think that way. If you say something harsh or insulting to another person, and you don't want to hear their response, you can just block that person, delete them, or shut your computer off. You can avoid the conflict you started!

What is really interesting about online social networking is the degree of impersonal representation people have of online friendships. Since many people view their internet experiences as occurring as a by-product or function of their computer—which in essence occurs because of synthetic microchips—many view people online and their experiences with them as "synthetic" as well. I asked some people who frequent or are even addicted to these online social networking forums, "How real do you take these sites?" and many told me, not very real. In fact, some told me they use them for "entertainment" or to vent (i.e., say things online that they wouldn't dare do in the real world). What I often heard people saying was, "It's not like I am ever going to meet this person for real as they live on the other side of the world!"

If that isn't enough, some people state they make up fake personas or "aliases" online to try out personalities, or aspects of a personality they would like to try in the real world. What was really disturbing is that I had a couple of people tell me that they like to be "hacks" online: using the internet to argue or intentionally hurt others to get some sort of satisfaction for having been hurt or bullied by other people in the real world. Now that is very disturbing behaviour!

The other aspect to online social networking is instant gratification. When I refer to instant gratification I am referring to saying or doing something immediately online and not having to worry that there will be consequences. Furthermore, since many people don't consider the online forums and the people on them as real, they have little regard for the feelings of others. In the real world you would think people would act using their critical sensory filters and think before speaking. Online, there seems to be no rules: say what you want and don't worry about whether or not others will be hurt by what you are saying! Sad as it sounds, but there is too much of this going on in the cyber world.

In the last chapter, I suggest taking a short quiz to find out if you possess texting rage. Now we will look at online social networking anger/rage. Do you possess it? To find out whether or not you possess some or a lot of aspects of this type of rage, please take a few moments to engage in the following questionnaire:

1) I find that one of the first things that I do when I wake up in the morning is I either have to check my online social networks like Facebook, Twitter, etc., and if I don't I feel like I am missing out on something.

5 - Always
3 - Almost Always
1 - Sometimes
0 - Never

2) The longer I stay on my online social network site(s) each day, the more I find myself getting frustrated, even angry, with people on there.

5 - Always
3 - Almost Always
1 - Sometimes
0 - Never

3) In the last six months, I have found myself looking to start or get into arguments on online social network sites.

5 - Always
3 - Almost Always
1 - Sometimes
0 - Never

4) I find myself getting caught up in other peoples' drama on my online social network(s), or I find I have to remove people from them more often lately.

5 - Always

3 - Almost Always
1 - Sometimes
0 - Never

5) I have been blocked by several people and not allowed to be their "friend" on their social networks, and this is continually happening.

5 - Always
3 - Almost Always
1 - Sometimes
0 - Never

6) I have been warned by moderators or even banned by them for being argumentative, threatening or even abusive on online social network sites.

5 - Always
3 - Almost Always
1 - Sometimes
0 - Never

7) When I get offline from my social network site(s), I find myself getting into arguments quite easily in the real world as I already feel frustrated and now feel easily provoked.

5 - Always
3 - Almost Always
1 - Sometimes
0 - Never

8) I like going into online social network sites because I feel more superior, powerful or confident there versus the opposite in my real life.

5 - Always
3 - Almost Always
1 - Sometimes

0 - Never

9) I find it very easy to make abusive comments (e.g. sexist, racist or stereotypical) online as I know that no one can hurt me or touch me.

5 - Always
3 - Almost Always
1 - Sometimes
0 - Never

10) If I am having a bad day, I find it cathartic (relieving) or even entertaining to take it out on people online.

5 - Always
3 - Almost Always
1 - Sometimes
0 - Never

The highest total you could score is 50! If you scored 50, there is no doubt that you have an anger/rage tied to online social network sites like Facebook, Twitter, etc. After speaking with a large number of people who use these forums, and who have experienced anger as a result of being on there a lot, I came to these common scores or standards which may assert one has an anger problem tied to their online social networking:

40-50 ONLINE SOCIAL NETWORK RAGE
29-39 ADVANCED ONLINE SOCIAL NETWORK RAGE
19-28 GETS FRUSTRATED EASILY USING ONLINE NETWORKING

9-18 SOME FRUSTRATION USING ONLINE NETWORKING
0-8 COULD CARE LESS ABOUT USING ONLINE NETWORKING

If you scored 29 or above, you might want to consider that you have some issues surrounding communication that is inclusive of technology. It is interesting to point out that even though many people possess this online social networking rage, they do not have it in their everyday conversational interactions when it comes to face to face communication.

Another salient point I came upon while doing research for this book is regarding rules and protocol. Much like texting, there are no real rules. The rules you think would apply are rules that people carry around with them from the real world in terms of how they communicate and interact with others. Facebook seemed to have a tremendous mystique surrounding itself with how folks should treat one another, what they should post on their "walls" and also, who they should add.

I came across many people, especially those e-mailing me after I appeared on a series of radio shows in Top 35 markets across the USA. I did a series of talk shows on Facebook and the rules/obligations for adding people that are your ex-lovers or acquaintances of your current mate. To be honest, I couldn't believe this tremendous can of worms could be occurring all because of a former mate or spouse being added. Furthermore, I couldn't believe how many people have been or were currently being "stalked" or "spied" on Facebook!

Here is a partial list of some of the situations I was made aware of, and even counselled:

1) My ex spouse wants me to add them, or I already "friended" them on my Facebook page and my current mate is irate about it.

2) My spouse/mate who is a "friend" on my page questions me, or watches my Facebook page for conversations they are not a part of.

3) Other people post things on my wall that are degrading, humiliating or create sensitivity to me or my mate.

4) Whenever I post something funny or even somewhat serious, other people post critical remarks or create undo drama on my Facebook page.

5) Some of the people I added on my Facebook page continually try to add my friends, and this is making my friends angry because they do not even know them.

6) Some people constantly change their relationship status from "single" to "in a relationship" and so forth because they love the attention.

7) Some people continually remove themselves from someone's Facebook page after they felt slighted or ignored, only to beg to be added back.

8) People posted derogatory things about others on Facebook and Twitter when that individual was not around and could not delete or answer the posting.

9) Some people actually sent another person an internet virus to disable their computer!

10) Some people created aliases or fake names to get added back onto someone's online social networking page.

One of the most common and disturbing incidences, when it comes to online networking and rage, involves exes or estranged mates. It seems even though a couple physically split (divorce, separation, or move out), they are still in each other's lives as they remain "friends" on Facebook pages, or their children's/friend's pages where they can still see the goings-on of the other or still take vengeful jabs at the other person. I don't have hard facts or stats on it, but I am going to guess just as there are restraining orders put on individuals when a marriage goes bad in real life, there are likely ones for online social networking.

More kids and teens are using online social networking to bully their peers. I mentioned earlier on how I have been involved with several anti-bullying campaigns and self esteem-building events to help kids, parents, teachers and law enforcement deal with this phenomenon. The internet has become a "safe haven" for people from all walks of life, especially kids, to take stabs and attack others. They know they can hide behind the safety of their computer and not face any consequences—well at least not now, but the law is cracking down in more countries on this. Back in the day—actually when I was a kid—teen and young adult bullying that occurred in schools and workplaces were face-to-face.

Interestingly, workplace, domestic violence, and school violence is more passive-aggressive in nature. In *What's Your Anger Type?* , I cover passive-aggressive personality in great depth as to why it occurs and how to deal with people like that. For the purpose of keeping things brief here, I will describe passive-aggression as possessing the following attributes:

1) You never tell the person to their face what you are really feeling or thinking.

2) You often times pretend that everything is okay.

3) If the other person asks you if anything is wrong, you deny there is.

4) Inside you are angry and bitter because you do not get what you really want and the people you are dealing with don't usually get what they want.

5) No one feels comfortable in conflict situations being around you, including yourself.

6) You may say you forgive, but you don't and you sure as heck do not forget!

7) You motto is "I don't get mad, I get even!" and often you are looking for that opportunity to "get even"!

As sad as it may sound, the internet and social networking sites have provided passive-aggressive people with that "opportunity" to get even. By the way, they may say they don't get mad, but that is a lie! They are more than mad; they are scorned and they definitely want to even things up.

When bullying is not done face to face, how is it done online? I have found that often the physical bullying is carried out online through physical threats. With that said, too many people—the ones doing the threatening—are aware of laws and getting into trouble for uttering threats. As a result, they have changed their method of operation and do so in more subtle and less threatening manners. Let's face it: abuse is still abuse!

Some of the more prevalent kinds of online abuse come in the form of emotional/psychological abuse, sexual abuse and spiritual abuse. When I do lectures and workshops on violence, bullying and abuse, I break down the types as follows so people can see they may be similar in some areas, but very distinct in others. In essence then, there are various ways individuals can be abused or feel abused by being around others. These would include any of the following:

1) **Physical Abuse**

The actual act of hitting someone physically or threatening them physically would constitute physical abuse. Also, hindering an individual from going somewhere or slowing their progress during a work assignment would also be a form of physical abuse. What if a co-worker plays their music too loud, smokes at their work site against regulation, or creates some environmental hazard or obstacle? Physical Abuse!

2) **Emotional/Psychological Abuse**
The act of threatening someone or creating tension and stress in someone's life against their will can be considered emotional abuse. Placing unrealistic expectations on someone or even denying them the opportunity to fulfill a goal also qualifies. Discrimination based on race, religion, gender, ideology and age (ageism) can be considered forms of these types of abuse. Stalking someone online, harassment, name calling, being a burden are all emotional/psychological abuse.

3) **Sexual Abuse**
The act of touching someone in a sexually explicit manner is considered sexual abuse, e.g., touching, fondling, grabbing, frotteurism, molesting, kissing, caressing, rape, etc. Sexual harassment is also a form of sexual abuse. To make indecent remarks based on gender or sexuality to elicit a shock response or personal gratification is wrong. Telling sexually-laden jokes or making "cat calls" can also be considered forms of sexual abuse. To send indecent or sexually-crude pictures to someone online is sexual abuse, as well as posting character defamation comments or pictures based on sexuality.

4) **Spiritual Abuse**
To be discriminated against or mocked because of one's religious or spiritual beliefs can be considered forms of spiritual abuse. To deny someone their religious holiday, which is regularly observed, is a form of this abuse. To send racist or religious jokes

can also be considered abusive. Finally, trying to brainwash someone for the purpose of inducing them to join a cult, can also be considered spiritual abuse. Interestingly, a religious denomination who tells its members to give up respectable jobs or education, or they will be disowned by the religion or family can also be considered a form of spiritual abuse.

I have provided a very large overview to distinguish the various types of bullying and acts of aggression. Even though many people spend a large part of their day in front of computers, they are not immune from these types of aggression coming their way. In fact, they might even be the perpetrators of these acts of aggression.

What can you do to deal with or stop online social networking rage or not get caught up in it either as a perpetrator of aggression or the victim? Here is a list of some simple rules to follow:

RULE #1
Always know who you are adding to your online social networking lists/friend pages, as well as know who you are talking to. If you do not know someone who is trying to start an argument with you, or are suspicious of them, cut off the communication.

RULE #2
Don't spend too much time online social networking to the point where you are getting bored or frustrated. When you get to this level of tedious frustration, you are more likely to start venting and rather than beat on your keyboard or monitor, you

are more likely to be harsh with people you are talking with.

RULE #3

If you are starting a new relationship, it is probably not a good idea to add your new mate to your networks such as Facebook, especially if you have exes on them. The idea of adding or having ex mates on your Facebook page and the ramifications is a whole other book. With that said, you may have a comfortable amicable relationship with your ex on Facebook that your new mate does not understand and the last thing you would want them to do is misconstrue a comment they read or become suspicious.

RULE #4

Don't let online social networking interfere with your relationships (spouse, family, friends, etc.), or your work or professional career. The problem is when the online life spills into your real life, bringing online frustrations with you. Just as you might vent your everyday frustrations to the people on the internet, you may do the reverse to your real life.

RULE #5

Always try to communicate online with a cool head and mild disposition. Remember that once you post something and it goes viral, there is no taking it back. Sometimes the harshest things we say and do happen when we are angry. After the fact, we wish we could take it back. To say or do something mean online is stored online!

RULE #6
If you are ever uncertain of an intended message from another person online, seek to clarify it. Never jump to conclusions. If you can send the person a private message or call them over the phone, then do so immediately to clarify whatever is misunderstood, or resolve the problem. Also, never post anything that is sent to you that you are unsure of, or do not have the complete facts.

RULE #7
Never post anything that is private (i.e., details about your house, career, family, etc.) online in the social networks. Also, avoid putting detailed pictures of your home as well as pictures of your kids and valuables. The last thing you want to do is really tee someone off and have them use it against you or, in some cases, burglarize your home or by sharing and "tagging" photos of you and passing them on virally.

These are simple and very basic rules for online social networking which could help save you a lot of headache and grief. Unfortunately many people get caught up in not only the novelty of online social networking; they also get addicted to it! This only adds to their frustration and before they know it, they type something they will regret. Learn to treat people online the same way you would in your everyday world, hopefully the way you would want others to treat you!

CYBERDATING

It's 2016 and it seems that most dating is done in a techno-domain: INTERNET DATING! Text messaging and internet dating literally go hand in hand these days...ah, dating in the palm of your hand! When my co-author Dr. Debra Laino (sex therapist) and I were researching/writing our book *The Madonna Complex: Why Men Are Wired To Cheat*, some men were not only addicted to the "sexting" but also internet dating sites!

Most people enter into the world of internet dating with the goal of finding that special someone, or at least a friend...someone they can trust. Many online dating users believe it is like placing an order and waiting for their match to just show up. In the beginning, it is fun because it is a novel experience. Some theorists say that it takes 21 to 28 days to become habituated to a vice or addiction if you do it every day in that period. If you are using internet dating for that time period, there is a good chance that you are probably getting hooked, if not addicted to it. Yikes! Now with the World Wide Web in the palm of your hand, you can cyber date anytime and anywhere. For some, this becomes text message dating and that becomes their new addictive behaviour. The one thing I learned from people who are at this level of usage, in terms of needing to constantly date online, is that they become addicted to the attention they are receiving.

ATTENTION! Most people love the attention they get: someone is thinking about them, communicating with them, flirting with them, making them feel special or is being intimate with them through sexting. And to follow up "attention", many stated that this venue for dating works so well because you don't have to put too much effort into it. Conversely, some did say it is very costly in terms of wasting time or being distracted from what they should be doing—work—because they are addicted to their text dating. Then comes their frustration...

You see most people began internet dating with the purpose of meeting someone special for "love". They had the best of intentions, as did most using internet dating, but the longer you try something and not succeed, the more likely you are to become frustrated. I believe this frustration is a by-product of perceived failure. Let's face it, if you are doing something long enough, over and over, and not getting the results you are seeking, then that means you are not succeeding. If you are not succeeding then it means that you must be failing! Realistically speaking, most people take failure personally, especially when it is based on what you believe to be rejection. Ever wonder what failure—which becomes equated with rejection—must mean to many who are internet dating and getting nowhere? ANGER! I had many people call it another term: INSANITY. They believed they were insane for not only engaging in it still, but doing the same thing expecting different results.

In the end, we are social creatures needing acceptance, love, and to feel desired by someone, especially if we are single. Since internet dating is anonymous and even secretive for the most part, some people push the envelope a little too far, too fast to get the attention they desire from others. And just as text messaging causes miscommunication and short-comings to understanding, internet dating experiences leave many confused, bewildered, insulted and even feeling unfulfilled! It's the last point which gets many into trouble as they become desensitized and need to take things to a new, non-cyber level. The anger and frustration they are feeling from on-line dating spills out into their everyday lives, and are most likely to take it out in the real world. Furthermore, I had several people tell me that even when they are meeting people from online dating, they are already jaded, or have a negative expectation about the date as they have been disappointed, burnt or hurt enough times already. They literally expect the worst!

In abusive relationships, there is a concept known as Object Relations Cycle. This is based on the awesome work of David Celani, who examined why women return to abusers who continually abuse or cheat on them. Why would someone return to an abusive individual? Moreover, why would an abuser take someone back who is a pushover? In Object Relations Cycle there are two roles the individual places: The Hopeful Self and the Abused Self.

The Hopeful Self is the part of the persona an abused or frustrated carries around with them. They believe things will change even though it doesn't look like it will. Don't get me wrong: hope is a great thing to have and we should all have it. With that said, hope is only good when you are able to rise out of a negative situation and seek or bring about positive change. If the situation is the same, abuse/frustration are a constant and will be in that situation, you can be as hopeful as heck, but unless you see the situation for what it is, or act the same way according to the situation, things will remain status quo—you know... insanely doing the same thing and expecting a different outcome?

The hopeful self in an abusive relationship hopes that the abuse will stop. When her mate promises he will change for the umpteenth time, and he even shows some signs of it, the hopeful self kicks in and all is "merry" for a while. This is also known as the "honeymoon" stage or "chocolate and hearts" phase where the abuser is on their best behaviour. If the abuser is seeking counseling, anger management, and working support groups to bring about change, then this is a great thing as they believe they possess a problem and are seeking to change for themselves. If they are doing it for their spouse—to save the relationship or face—then it will not work, as they are doing it for all of the wrong reasons. They will revert back to their abusive ways in just a matter of time, when some triggering event imprinted on their unconscious will set them off. They will blame their mate or someone else for this and the cycle of abuse is most likely to start again. This is when the abused self kicks in...

Because he "blames" her for becoming angry and abusive again, many women who are abused believe it is her fault. He tells her he was doing better, being non-abusive and getting "help", so it must be her fault the abuse happened. Some people who develop a sense of learned helplessness, possess low self-esteem and even feel like a perennial victim, truly believe this. This is the mindset of the "abused self" which asserts, "I must have done something to deserve this!". Of course this thinking is wrong, destructive and irrational! When you put two irrational people together—an abuser and the one being abused—their thinking patterns which lead to their feelings and eventual actions are irrational. When they are both in the abusive mode, they are operating in their Abused Self mindsets. When they are trying to make things better or seeking reconciliation, this then shifts to the hopeful self and then things become fine and dandy.

The reason I provided this discussion on the hopeful and abused selves, is I believe this same phenomenon is occurring in online dating. After speaking with many people who are using it—as well as those who volunteered information to a question I posed in an online social networking site—I am convinced many people are caught up in this conundrum! Let me explain...

The longer you engage in the online dating sites and get poor results, leading to frustration and thus taking it personally, you begin to shift into an abused self mode. You can go one of two ways with this: either everyone is a "loser" and "out to waste mine and everyone else's time", or "I am too good for everyone and no one is going to meet my expectations".

In the beginning, you are in a hopeful self mindset: "This will be fun to date, to hopefully meet the person of my dreams!"; "This shouldn't be difficult: so many people to choose from, all here like me to meet someone!"; and "This is easy; I don't even have to go to a bar, or work hard at this in a physical sense as I can do it all from my computer!" is what most people using online dating reported. After months of lack of success, getting the run around and being disappointed—that is, for a large contingent I spoke with—they started to get frustrated. This is when the abused self mindset starts the shift. You wonder, "Will I ever meet someone of quality?"; "Is everyone out here a player?"; or "Am I always going to get the run-around?" Remember the 21 to 28 days habit and addiction cycle. You may be fed up with online dating, but you just can't seem to quit as it has become a lifestyle, habit or dare I say addiction?

When the frustration dissipates a bit, or you learn of someone having success with online dating, or there is some sort of trigger that gives you a sense of renewed hope, then you shift back into the hopeful self mindset: "This time it is going to work, I just know it!". And if it doesn't, I think you know how the cycle goes.

In the last chapter, I suggested taking a short quiz to find out if you possessed online social networking rage. Now we will look at online dating anger/rage. Do you possess it? To find out whether or not you possess aspects of this type of rage or a lot of this rage, please take a few moments to engage in the following questionnaire:

1) I find that I cannot go one day without logging in or having to check an online dating site.

5 - Always
3 - Almost Always
1 - Sometimes
0 - Never

2) Whenever I use online dating, I find myself getting frustrated the longer I am on it.

5 - Always
3 - Almost Always
1 - Sometimes
0 - Never

3) I tend to think of the people using online dating as being mostly jerks and players.

5 - Always
3 - Almost Always
1 - Sometimes
0 - Never

4) I find myself getting into arguments with people I have never met whenever I use online dating.

5 - Always
3 - Almost Always
1 - Sometimes
0 - Never

5) I find it easy to be rude to people using online dating because I am not face to face with them and never plan on meeting them.

5 - Always
3 - Almost Always
1 - Sometimes
0 - Never

6) I tend to take my frustration and anger out on people using online dating as my real life dating successes are lacking.

5 - Always
3 - Almost Always
1 - Sometimes
0 - Never

7) I believe if I contact someone using online dating, then they should always have the decency to at least respond back.

5 - Always
3 - Almost Always
1 - Sometimes
0 - Never

8) When people ignore me or are rude to me who use online dating, I get very angry.
5 - Always
3 - Almost Always
1 - Sometimes
0 - Never

9) I tend to always check up on certain individuals using the online dating sites who have rejected me just to see if they are online still.
5 - Always
3 - Almost Always
1 - Sometimes
0 - Never

10) I have created other accounts or aliases when using online dating just to play someone or hurt them because they hurt or rejected me.
5 - Always
3 - Almost Always
1 - Sometimes
0 - Never

The highest total you could score is 50! If you scored 50, there is no doubt that you have an anger/rage tied to online dating. After speaking with a large number of people who use online dating, and who have experienced anger as a result of being on there a lot, I came to these common scores or standards which may assert one has an anger problem tied to their online dating experiences:

40-50 ONLINE DATING RAGE

29-39 ADVANCED ONLINE DATING RAGE

19-28 GETS FRUSTRATED EASILY USING ONLINE DATING

9-18 SOME FRUSTRATION USING ONLINE DATING

0-8 COULD CARE LESS ABOUT USING ONLINE DATING

If you scored 29 or above, you might want to consider for yourself that you have some issues surrounding communication that is inclusive of technology. It is interesting to point out that even though many people possess this online dating rage, they do not have it in their everyday conversational interactions when it comes to face-to-face communication. Some told me that their online dating experiences usually bring out the worst in them!

In my popular book *FAST FOOD DATING YOUR 2 CENTS*, my co-authors and I interviewed over a thousand people who used internet dating. We wanted to know the most common negative things about it and what set them off. Here is an excerpt from it:

This book would not be complete unless we listed some of the worst or negative attributes people have experienced when using Internet dating. Once again, they are not in any order, they are all just plain bad! **TOP 10** bad things about internet dating we found through our interrogations:

1) People posting pictures from previous decades, even centuries as representations of themselves today.
2) Exaggerate their body type, size and shape which is hard as heck to extrapolate from a head shot alone.
3) Height. What happened to the other five to six vertical inches you claimed to have?
4) Damn, on the internet you didn't have bad breath!

5) Posted ages off by anywhere between five to 10...even 20 years!
6) Married men pretending to be single.
7) Failure to realize that chatting on internet dating services doesn't actually constitute a true career.
8) Playing people by chatting on the internet and pretending to actually want to meet for real.
9) Here today/this moment and gone forever.
10) Difficult to read into people's messages due to lack of expression and not being able to look into one's eyes or read facial expressions. Damn...No polygraphs!

We were interested in knowing what were the three biggest peeves surrounding internet dating. If you could pick any three, what were they? Incidentally, the respondents reported pretty much the same ones as their **TOP 3**.

1) People lying about who and what they say they are.
2) Never a real intention to meet for real.
3) Why do all the good ones live in another country?

After reading this excerpt, do you still want to use online dating? Okay, perhaps you do, but don't want the anger associated with it. With that said here are some basic rules which I learned from people who successfully used online dating and were able to remain cool, calm and collected:

RULE #1

Never spend more than 45 to 60 minutes at a time online dating. The longer you are on, the more tedious and frustrating you are likely to become.

RULE #2
Limit the amount of hours online dating per day. Some asserted to keep it at no more than two hours or it could become very addictive, or used to procrastinate doing other activities, which might even include getting out of the person you are chatting with online.

RULE #3
Make the transition to talking on the phone or meeting in person. Too many people spend time online chatting with someone they have nothing in common with and find it frustrating and/or disappointing when they eventually meet the person and they are nothing like they projected them self to be and their fantasy bubble is burst.

RULE #4
Never give out home phone numbers, rather provide your cell number and if meeting, meet in a public place preferably in day light and let someone know where you are going. There are incidences of abuse, abductions, even murder linked to online dating as angry people with no morals or consciences use it to victimize people.

RULE #5
Never get into an online argument or conflict. It's not worth it as things can get misconstrued easily. Always seek clarification!

RULE #6
Never add anyone immediately from online dating forums to your other online social network forums. They might not be who you think they are and could cause you or others online harm.

RULE #7
Avoid using online dating whenever you are having a bad day or overtired. Just like real life, you may be off and say something you will later regret.

RULE #8
If and when someone rejects you or ignores you, don't take it personally. First off, they might not have gotten your message. Second, personalities differ and they might not have adequate skills. Third, they may feel they have nothing in common with you and do not want to turn you down. Fourth, that person may just be an idiot and they did you a favour.

RULE #9
No means no! Similar to Rule #8, if someone tells you they are not interested, or you meet and there is no connection, move on! The last thing you want to do is be persistent when instead it appears you are stalking them.

RULE #10
Don't force yourself on someone or pretend to be something you are not! Once you start to lie or deceive others, you will not only be frustrating to them but yourself as well in order to try and keep the deception going.

This is just a brief list of some of the things to watch for when using internet dating. Many people get caught up in not only the novelty of online dating, some get addicted to it! Just like the rules for online social networking, which are based on real life principles learn to treat people with respect and honesty!

Online dating anger is a very real phenomenon, just as texting rage and online social networking anger are too! People need to remember that they are still people: filled with human emotions even though they are communicating using technological devices, that are free of emotion. Keep this in mind: the person on the other end of the device or the one receiving the message you are sending is an emotional creature!

References

Movies:

Raging Bull
1980 Directed by Martin Scorsese

Single White Female
1992 Directed by Barbet Schroeder

The Talented Mr. Ripley
1999 Directed by Anthony Minghella

Books and Articles:

Heinz L. Ansbacher (1967). *The Individual Psychology of Alfred Adler: A Systematic Presentation in Selections from His Writings.* Harper & Row. New York. Library of Congress Catalog Number: 55-6679

Albert Bandura (1977). *Social Learning Theory,* Prentice-Hall, Englewood Cliffs. ISBN-13: 978-0138167448

Eric Berne (1964). *Games People Play: The Basic Handbook of Transactional Analysis.* ISBN-13: 978-0345410030

Margaret J. Black and Stephen A. Mitchell, (1995). *Freud and Beyond: A History of Modern Psychoanalytic Thought.* Basic Books. ISBN-13: 978-0465014057

Walter B. Cannon (1963). *The Wisdom of the Body*. Second edition, W. W. Norton. ISBN-13: 978-0393002058

Dale Carnegie (1994). *How to Win Friends & Influence People*. Vermilion. Revised ed. ISBN-13: 978-0749307844

David P. Celani (1994). *The Illusion of Love: Why the Battered Woman Returns to Her Abuser*. Columbia University Press. ISBN-13: 978-0231100373

Diagnostic and Statistical Manual of Mental Disorders - Fourth Edition (DSM-IV). The American Psychiatric Association (1994). Washington D.C ISBN-13: 978-0890420256

Albert Ellis and Arthur Lange, (1994). *How To Keep People From Pushing Your Buttons*. Carol Publishing Grp. ISBN-13: 978-1559722247

Edward Hoffman, (1997*). The Drive for Self: Alfred Adler and the Founding of Individual Psychology*. Perseus Publishing. ISBN-13: 978-0201441949

Dario Nardi, (2001). *Multiple Intelligences and Personality Type*. Telos Publications. ISBN-13: 978-0966462418

I.P. Pavlov, (1925). *"Twenty years of objective study of the higher nervous activity (behavior) of animals."* State publication, 3rd edition. Articles, Nos. 1, 2, 3, 4, 7, B, 10, 11, 13, 17, 20, 21, 23, 28, 29, 31, 33, 35.

Don Richard Riso and Russ Hudson, (2003). *Discovering Your Personality Type: The Essential Introduction to the Enneagram.* Mariner Books. ISBN-13: 978-0618219032

C.R. Rogers and R. Sanford, (1984). *Client-Centered Psychotherapy.* Constable. ISBN-13: 978-1841198408

Kaplan, H. and Sadock, B. (Eds.). *Comprehensive textbook of Psychiatry/IV.* pp. 1374-1388. Williams & Wilkins. ISBN-13: 978-0683045116

C.R. Rogers and B. Stevens, (1994). *Person to Person: The Problem of Being Human.* Souvenir Press. ISBN-13: 978-0285647176

H. Selye, (1978). *The Stresses Of Life.* McGraw Hill. ISBN-13: 978-0070562127

H. Selye, (1955). *Stress And Disease.* Science 1955; 122:625.

Bartlett H. Stoodley, (1959). *The Concepts of Sigmund Freud.* Free Press. Library of Congress Catalog Card No. 58-9401

Recommended Readings:

The Success Principles. Jack Canfield and Janet Switzer. ISBN-10: 0060594896 Harper Collins Publishers

Defining Mental Health As A Public Health Problem. William Glasser M.D. booklet, created to provide a new resource for mental health professionals.

Cracking The Millionaire Code. Mark Victor Hansen and Robert G. Allen. ISBN: 9781400082940 Harmony Books

Don't Throw Away Tomorrow. Robert H. Schuller. ISBN: 9780060563424 HarperCollins

Meditations For Overcoming Life"s Stresses And Strains. Bernie Siegel M.D. ISBN: 0060917059 Hay House

Not to People Like Us: The Hidden Abuse in Upscale Marriages. Dr. Susan Weitzman. ISBN-10: 0465090745 Basic Books

Children and Anger:

Defying the Defiance. Tip Frank, Mike Paget & Jerry Wilde. ISBN: 1889636770 Youthlight Inc.

Adult Children: The Secrets of Dysfunctional Families. John Friel. ISBN: 9780932194534 Deerfield Beach, Fla: Health Communications

Healthy Anger: How to Help Children and Teens Manage Their Anger. Bernard Golden. ISBN-10: 0195304500 Oxford University Press

Parenting the Explosive Child: The Collaborative Problem Solving Approach. Ross Greene & Stuart Ablon. ISBN-10: 1593852037 The Guilford Press

Other books by Peter Sacco

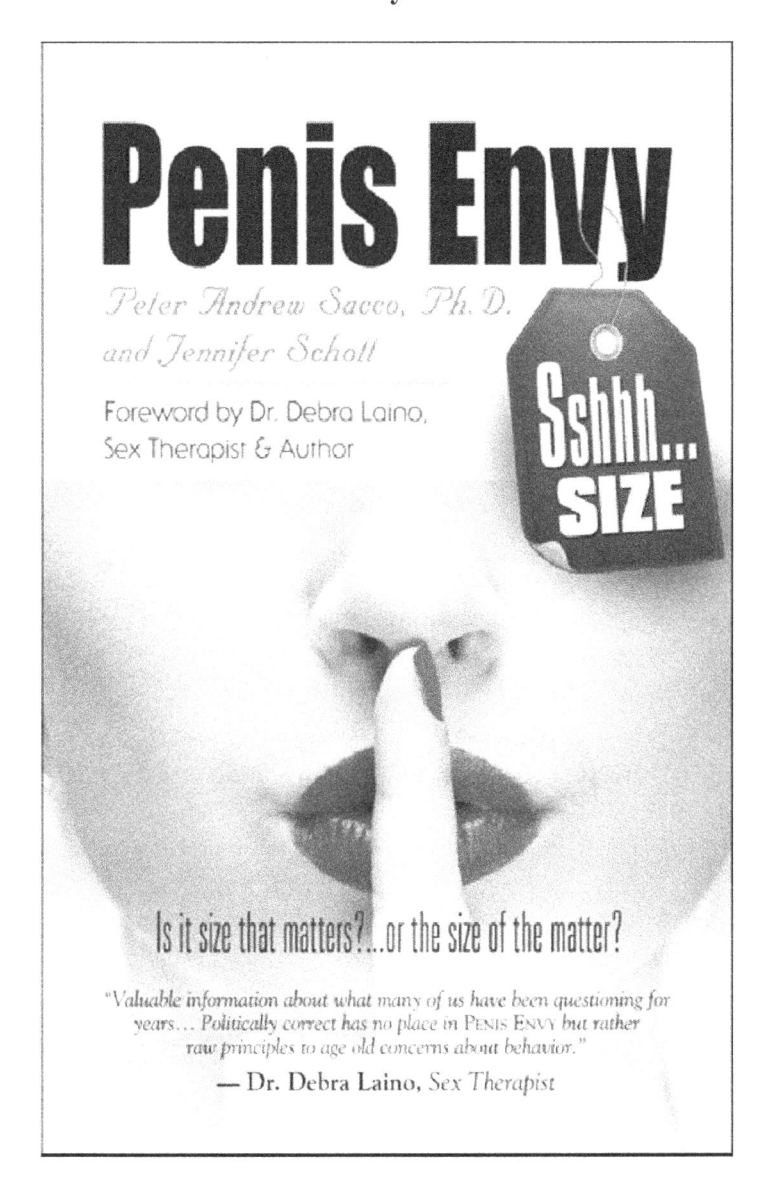

Penis Envy

Peter Andrew Sacco, Ph.D.
and Jennifer Schott

Foreword by Dr. Debra Laino,
Sex Therapist & Author

Sshhh... SIZE

Is it size that matters?...or the size of the matter?

"Valuable information about what many of us have been questioning for years... Politically correct has no place in PENIS ENVY but rather raw principles to age old concerns about behavior."

— Dr. Debra Laino, *Sex Therapist*

Take an informative journey through the world of gender differences and how they continue to hinder relationships and marriages.

- Why so many relationships continue to fail
- Why women settle for less than ideal mates
- Why women stay in bad relationships
- Why many men are threatened by change
- How to succeed in relationships and keep them alive.

"One of the best books I have read on the dynamics of relationships. ... A reading must for anyone who desires a healthy, well-balanced and satisfying relationship. Surely, that's everyone."

– Stephanie Nielsen, B.A., M.Ed.

"*In this book, Dr. Sacco helps by giving you a range of tools that can help you be successful.*"
— SANDERSON LAYNG, Vice President and Chief Operating Officer, Canadian Centre for Abuse Awareness

MAKING ADDICTIONS
A LASTING THING OF THE PAST!

RIGHT NOW ENOUGH IS ENOUGH!

OVERCOMING ADDICTIONS AND BAD HABITS
FOR GOOD IN 30 DAYS OR LESS!

Peter Andrew Sacco, PH.D.

To learn more about Peter Andrew Sacco and his work, or to book him for a speaking engagement, please visit his website:

www.petersacco.com